Praise for Windows

"Rapt observations of nature and people frame reflections on the human predicament in this luminous collection of poems and photographs.

Dornblaser's verse works in a range of registers and a fertile mixture of them, managing to be both scientific and lyrical in the same breath...and replete with visceral imagery. The result is a sumptuous feast for the mind and eye. A captivating synthesis of poetry and visuals, full of vibrant, resonant tableaux."

– Kirkus Reviews

"Windows blends nature photography and poetry in a visual and verbal exploration that tells of windows into other worlds, and taking the time to look through them.

Each poem is vividly portrayed, incorporating nature observation and employing color and descriptors that not just compliment the color images, but match their impact.

Dornblaser's powerful photos and written words are symphonies of experience, reflection, and observation inviting readers to look out the window of their own lives to experience their world in its fullest glory.

The intersections of man, nature, and a sense of place are clear. Look through Dornblaser's windows to receive observations that are life-affirming testimonies to connections between self and the world.

This rare view belongs in any poetry or arts lending library, and on the shelves of those who would follow the author on inner journeys and artistic observations."

– D. Donovan, Senior Reviewer, Midwest Book Review

Fire and Ice Photography
www.fireandicephoto.com
Louisville, Colorado, USA

First Edition published 2023

Windows
Library of Congress Control Number: 2021922805

I. Title: Windows
II. ISBN: 978-0-578-32054-0
1. Poems. 2. Prose Poems. 3. Photography.

Windows

Mark Dornblaser

*For Deb
my friend, my wife,
my love, my life.*

Contents

Foreword

When I make time to write, my muse prefers not to be summoned on a moment's notice. My brain needs time to ponder in peace, time to let an alphabet soup of words simmer on the stove, time to stare at the world until words begin to coalesce into fragments, fragments into lines, lines into poems.

Some years back, and without forethought, I found myself on a plane with nothing to do – no book, no music, no movie – and by looking out my airplane window for a while, I found words stewing in my head. This is the genesis of my book. It was the beginning of a realization that time alone could be found on an airplane – or in the case of some of the other poems in this collection, on a Greyhound bus from Minneapolis to Madison, in a hotel room in La Crosse, Wisconsin, during a long car ride from Denver to Minneapolis, sitting alongside Boulder Creek in Colorado, or standing in the surf on the Outer Banks.

Thus, windows are the theme of this book. As a poet and photographer, I look out through my own window, my own prism, to describe the human experience and the visual world. We all share in this human experience - what is our relationship with ourselves, our family and friends, and this beautiful world we live in? How do we adapt to a changing planet, and what does it mean to call someplace "home"? Can we find the peace that we seek, both individually and collectively?

Writing is sometimes a complicated and perplexing process. It is frustrating to search for the words that will convey the ideas in your head. As proof, I have numerous scraps of paper sitting in a folder for ideas that have yet to coalesce into a cohesive piece of writing. When a poem does come together, I find it magical. I wonder at the complexity of the human brain that disparate thoughts can gel into coherent ideas and imagery that are accessible and relatable to others.

That is my goal in sharing this work. It is immensely satisfying when I can make even a single connection to a reader of my poetry or viewer of my photography. Through windows, we look in upon ourselves, and gaze out into the world. Readers gazing out of their own windows may find commonalities in their own experiences with love, loss, regret, beauty, and hope. I'm hoping readers will enjoy joining me on this journey.

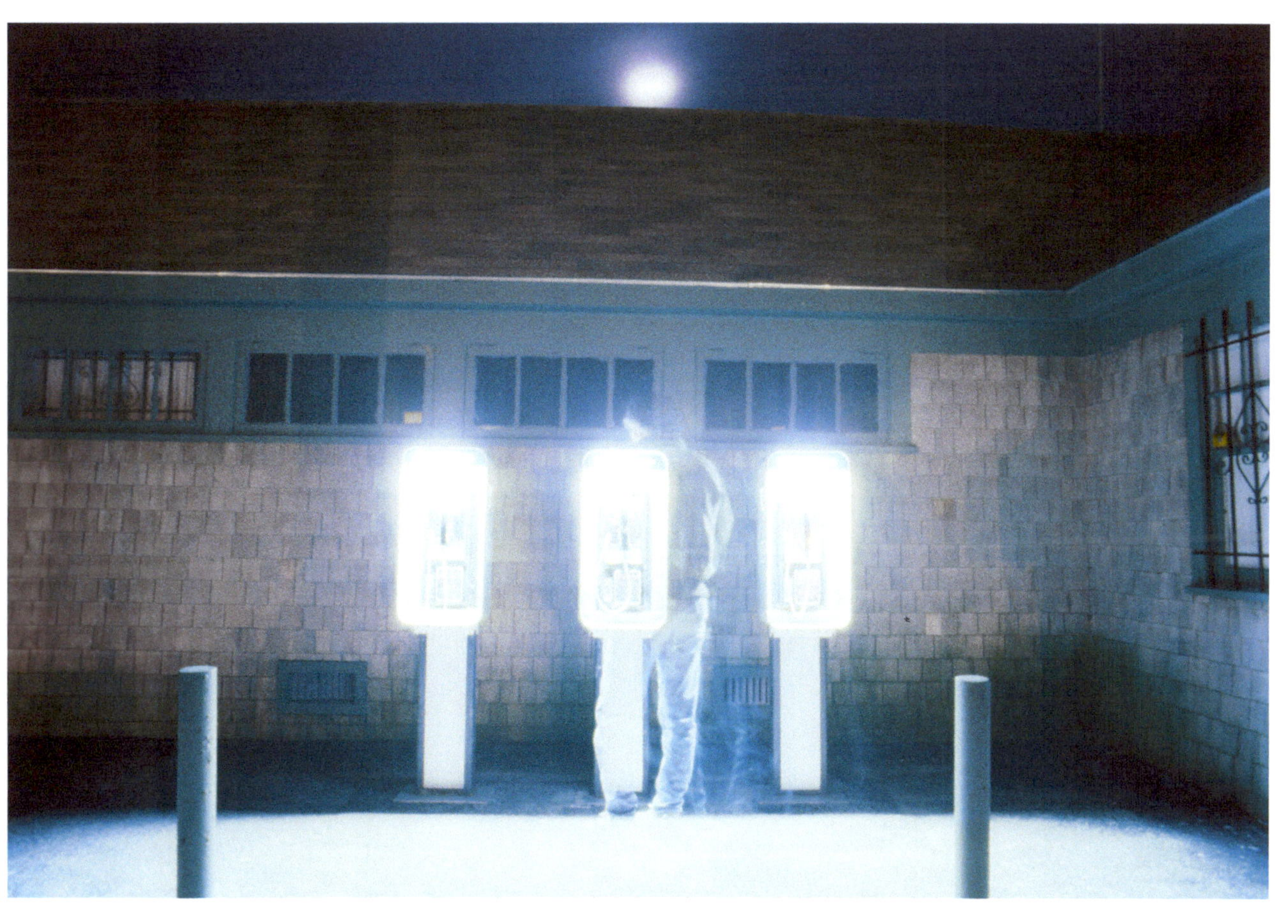

Self-portrait, Cape Cod, Massachusetts, circa 1987

Chapter 1 - Windows

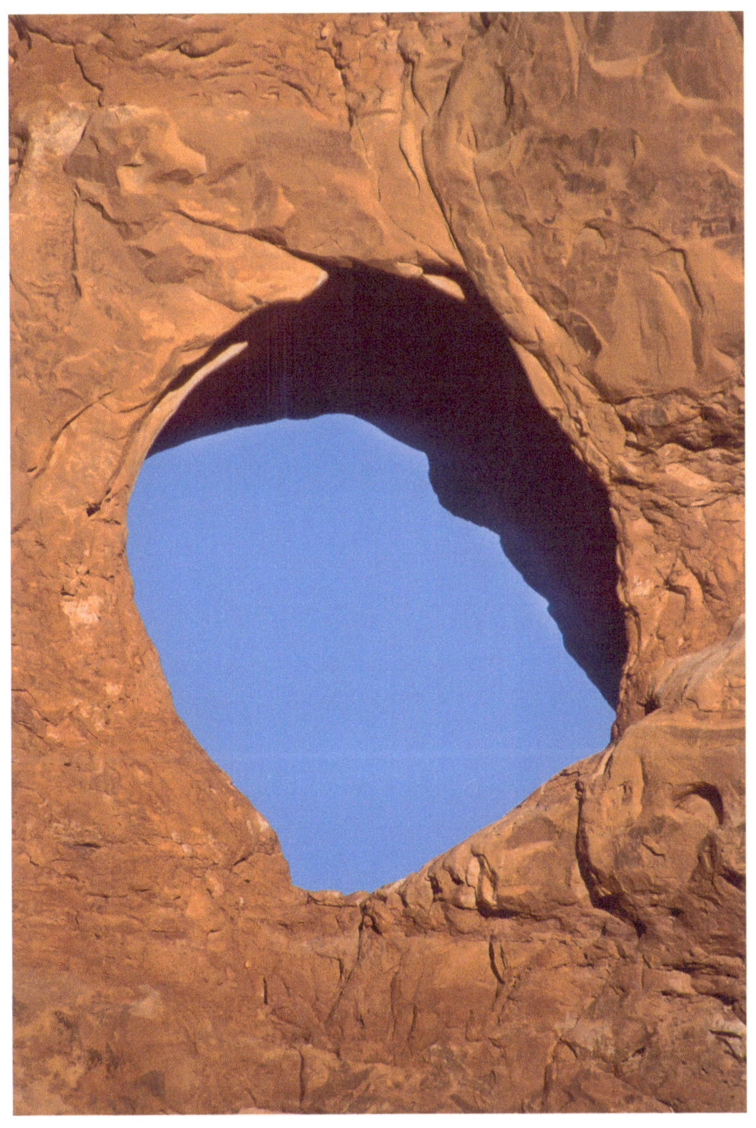

Scene from the Road

The early snowmelt seeps into the low seams of the fields,
a sinuous sheen of slate blue weaving through a rolling sea of white.
Islands of elm, oak, and birch, leafless,
cast long shadows across the late winter snow.
Cattle huddle around bales of hay,
breath freezing into frost.
A weathered, peeling barn is quiet,
and a rusting combine lies idle.
A silo stands watch over the outwash plains of east central Minnesota.

A waning moon hangs low over the horizon,
and a distant white steeple is the first to catch the straw-colored light of dawn.
Wisps of charcoal smoke rise straight and silent in the chill,
from a low-slung house at the end of the drive.
Out in the yard, a sodium light mounted on top of a steel pole switches off,
and I wonder, what illumination comes from within?

Windows

At night, the cities and towns below
resemble distant galaxies, or globular clusters,
slowly spinning assemblages of millions of stars,
connected by the invisible gravity of dark matter.

Lights from other planes
slide by silently in the darkness,
electrons energized into a higher orbital shell
above the nucleus of the earth.

Sinking lower, arcs of halogen headlights pulse
along avenues of energy, matter, and information,
speeding along concrete conduits,
carrying workers home at the end of the day.

Lower still, I can see lights on
in individual houses,
row by row,
block by block.

I picture the families
at the table eating dinner,
or children in their rooms doing homework,
or practicing the violin.

And upon hearing the jet above them,
do any, I wonder,
give pause at the window,
turn an ear to the sky,
think about the man seated in 28A,
and picture him gazing down upon their lives?

Sailing low across this ocean of night,
the lights flicker and fade behind me
like radioactive decay,
atoms breaking down,
electrons falling out of orbit,
just as I fall towards the solid ground
beneath these wings.

As we line up on the runway,
the landing lights, blinking in succession, point the way home.

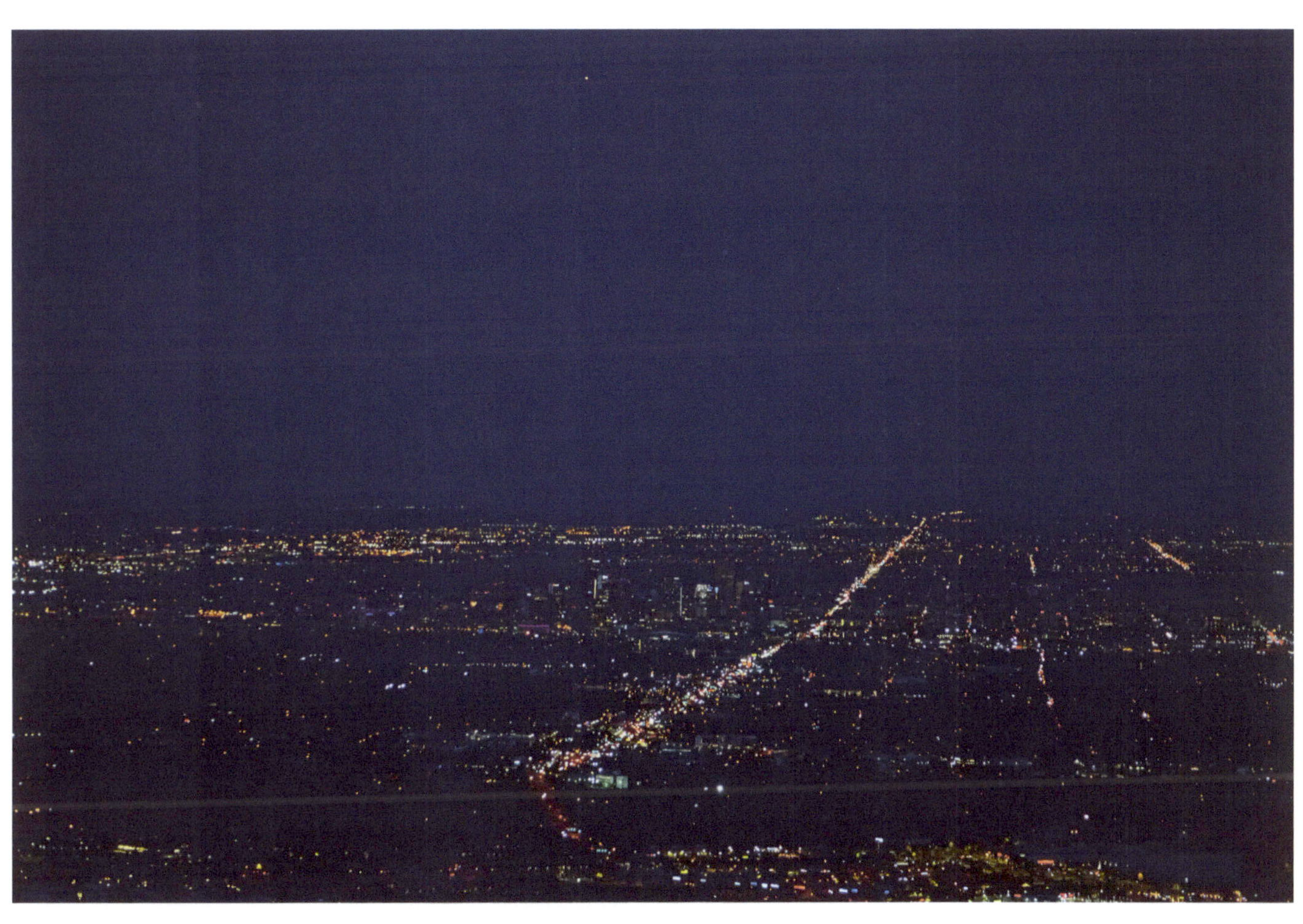

The Road

The road makes me weary.

Mile after mile ticks off, like the ticking of a clock.
I measure the rhythm of the road in the steady thumping of my tires passing over
seams in the concrete slabs, front wheels then rear in rapid succession,
like a heartbeat charged with adrenaline.

My eyes are tired, bloodshot and blind,
from scanning the road ahead in setting sun and halogen headlights.
With fuel running low in both tanks, I pull over in search of sleep.

I stare at the digital clock on the bedside table,
road shakes stirring me like unwanted caffeine.
Sodium light filters in through plastic curtains.
The A/C cycles on and off, the air cool but stale.
Big rigs drone by on the highway.

Footsteps rumble down the hall,
and a door clanks shut,
and a deadbolt flicks over,
and a chain slides into place.

I could be anywhere.
Which chain beds me down I can't remember.

*****

I pad across the ageing carpet, and splash cold water on my face.
In the lobby, strangers are coming and going, crossing paths in anonymity,
with perhaps a nod or hello or good morning at the coffee pot at breakfast,
the news in this faraway town too loud on the TV bolted up on the wall.

We go our separate ways,
some towards the rising sun,
some towards the waning moon.

We all return to the road.

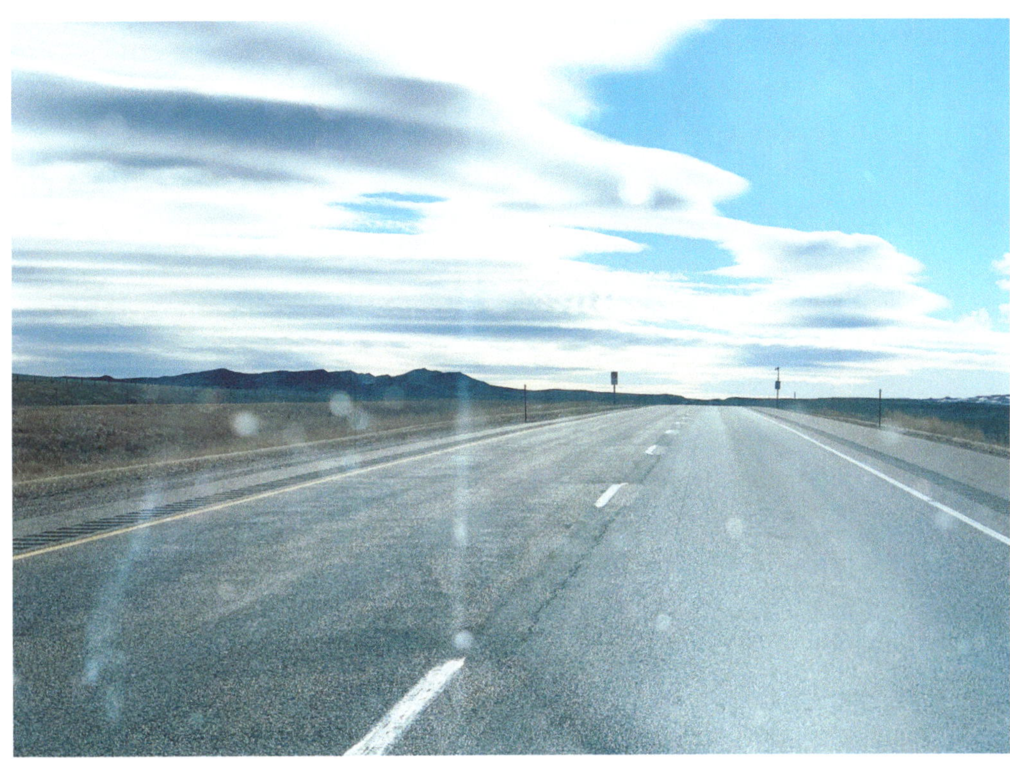

The Man

The man backs out of his driveway,
early, to catch the train. He passes
the garbage man, whistling while hefting barrels.
"Is he happier than I?" the man wonders.

At lunch on the corner, the server
pleasantly hands him his food.
"Are his dreams alive, are they simply lies,
or are they something worse?" the man asks.

On the evening train, he steals
glimpses of fellow travelers.
"Do their smiles mask
quiet desperation?" the man ponders.

Late at night the man listens
to his wife breathing beside him,
far away in dreams. He stares at dark shadows
falling on the floor.

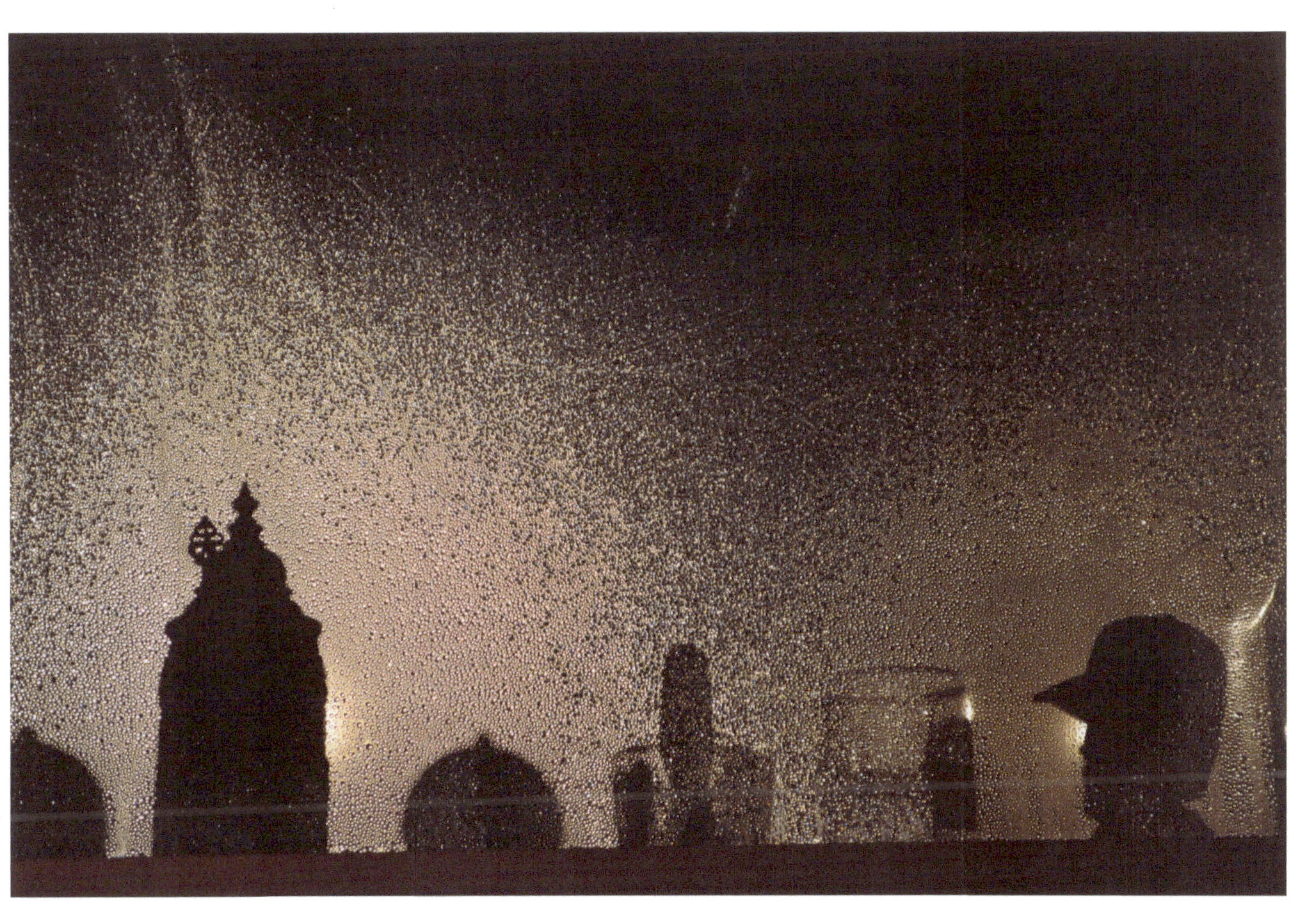

Cayman Blues

Cobalt coast,
cerulean sea,
indigo ocean,
they beckon me.

What dreams may come
on a rising tide,
follow me down
with you by my side.

Floating, flying,
finally free,
of the iron shore anchor
that drowns me.

Cayman blues
beneath my wings,
my return to the sea
one day will bring.

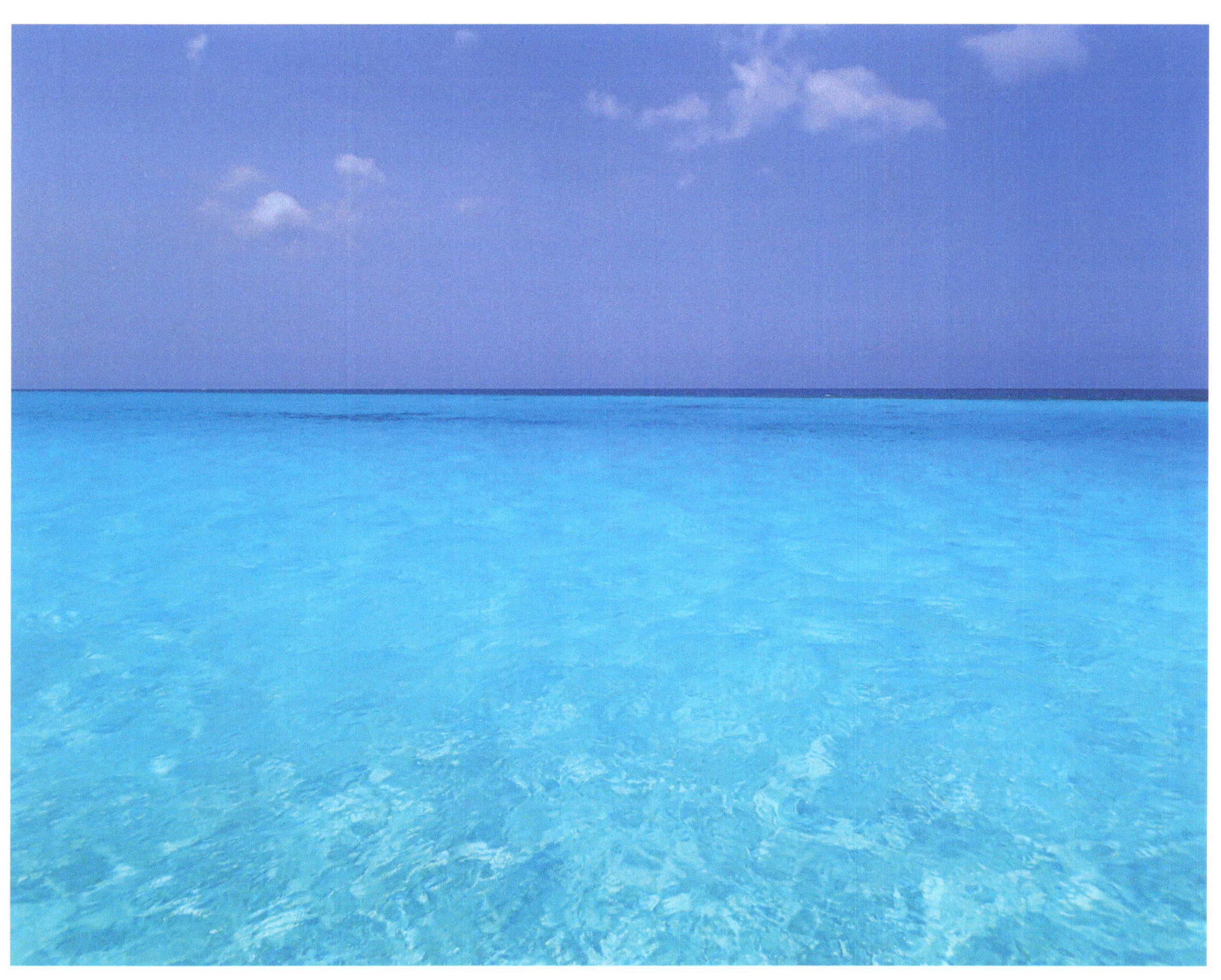

Friend Ships

At the airport this morning,
there is a 747 "Friend Ship" parked at a gate nearby.
This is her last stop before she is to be retired,
only one of a handful left.

Folks in the concourse take photos of her through the glass,
pale light rising in the east behind her.
On the tarmac, pilots and crew and other lucky souls
climb a small ladder and stand inside the engine cowling,
posing with smiles of remembrance of days gone by.

When she came to be she had lines that were like
nothing you'd seen before, and as a child I'd wonder
how such a big beautiful creature ever got off the ground.
In her heyday she was the "Queen of the Skies,"
when air travel was a pleasure,
when seats were roomy,
when meals were served,
when the smiles of the flight crew were easy,
because they didn't have to worry about
what might be hidden inside your shoes.

The Research Vessel Westward was
a gorgeous staysail schooner out of Woods Hole.
She had 125 feet of classic lines, 7000 square feet of sail,
and 36 souls aboard who became close friends.

She was retired too soon, I thought (and still think).
Surely, she had many more good years in her
(as I hope I have in me).
My goodbyes to her and my friends were too sudden.

Sometimes old friends slip away too easily,
like a ship sinking below the horizon, or retired to the boneyard.
They can enter your life unexpectedly,
yet at just the right time,
and become more important than you could have imagined.

The Age of Sail and the Magic of Flight of my youth are gone.

If you're lucky, sometimes you get one last chance
to say one more hello, and one last goodbye,
to old ships and old friends,
before they fade from view and memory,
to tell them how they found a place in your heart that will always remain.

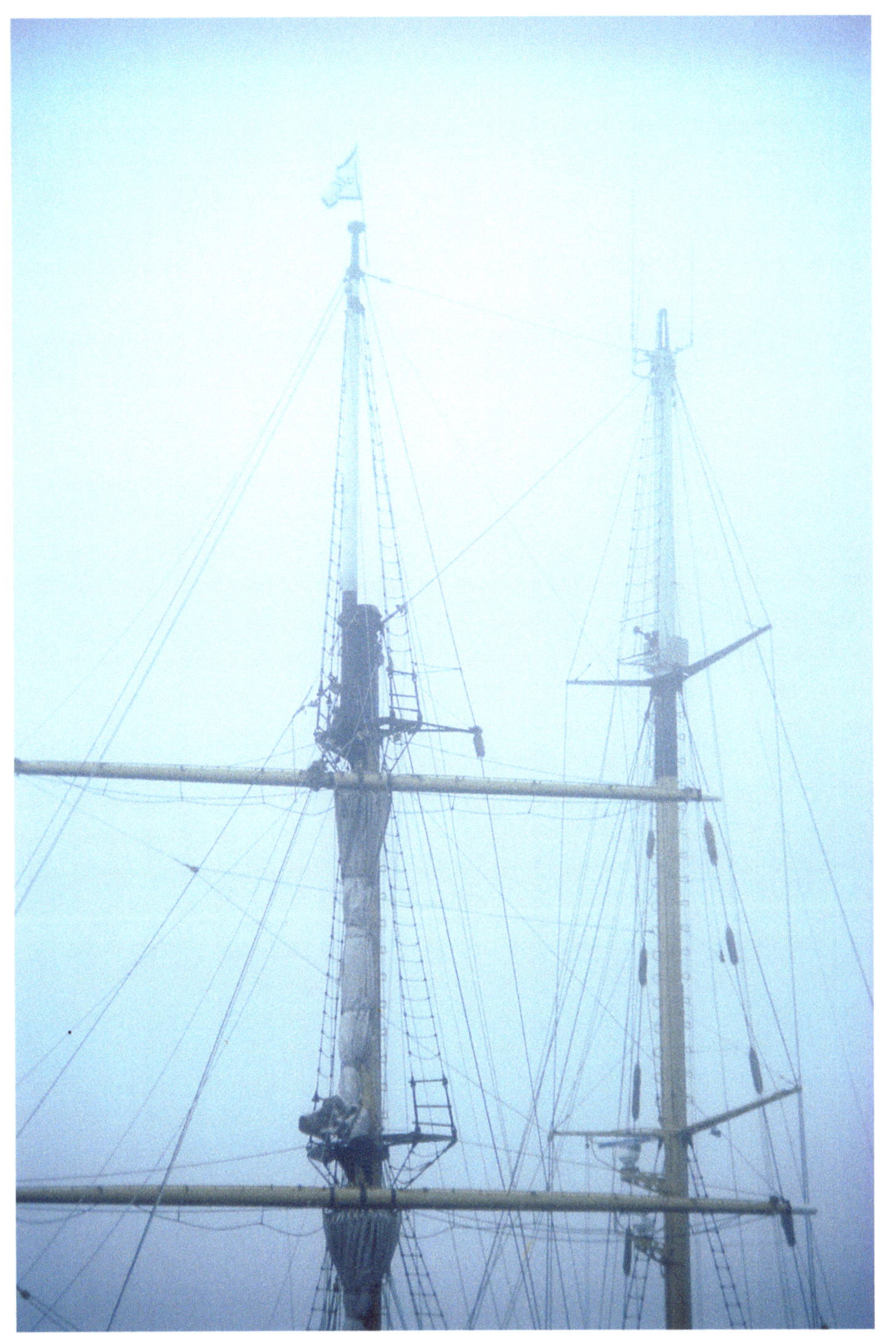

Chapter 2 - Love and Loss

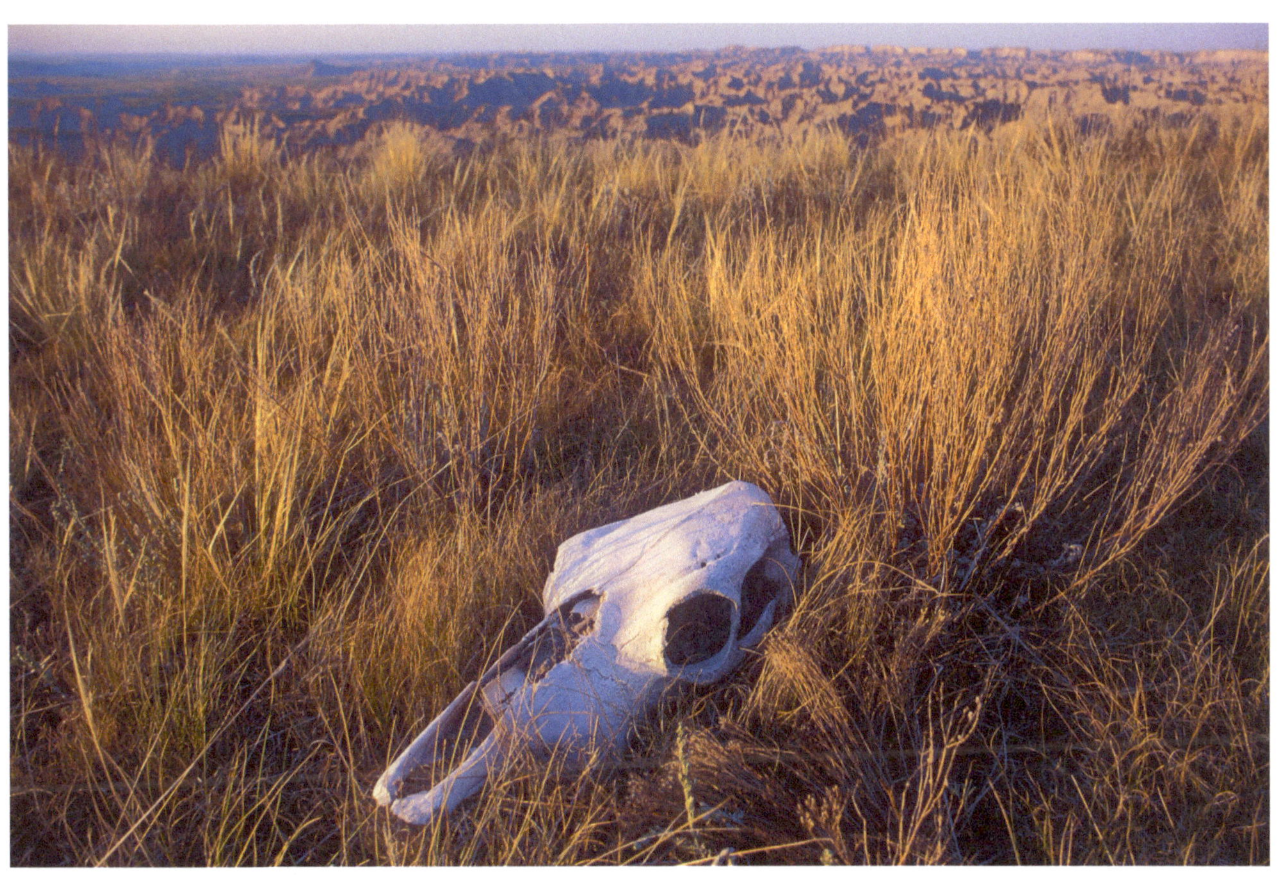

Skin

Driving across the Heartland,
back to Minnesota,
I stare at the thin fragile skin of land
that supports us.

Endless parallel furrows spin by
like spokes on a wheel.
Dig the right amount
and you can feed the world.
Dig too deep and hit
subterranean veins of rock,
or poisoned water that might flood the land.

Old wooden telephone poles
stand like crosses,
as if marking the dead in a long single file,
disappearing in fading light.

My father's skin is like dried parchment,
looking to slough off at the slightest breeze,
paper thin and easily bruised
from a steady supply of needles,
and bumps in the night.
Cut too deep and hit subcutaneous veins of blood and bone.

Sometimes I'd like to slip my skin,
but if I dig too deep beneath this hardened shell,
would I find the peace that I seek,
or simply a poisoned truth?

I return home again across the fields,
as sunset light paints a warm shaft of yellow
down a cold steel silo.
Drifts of snow sastrugi line the fence
at the edge of the barren winter field,
evidence of the restless winds
clawing and tearing at the earth's skin.

Rock and bone.
Water and blood.
Is there resilience enough in an old man's skin?
Is there resilience enough in mine?

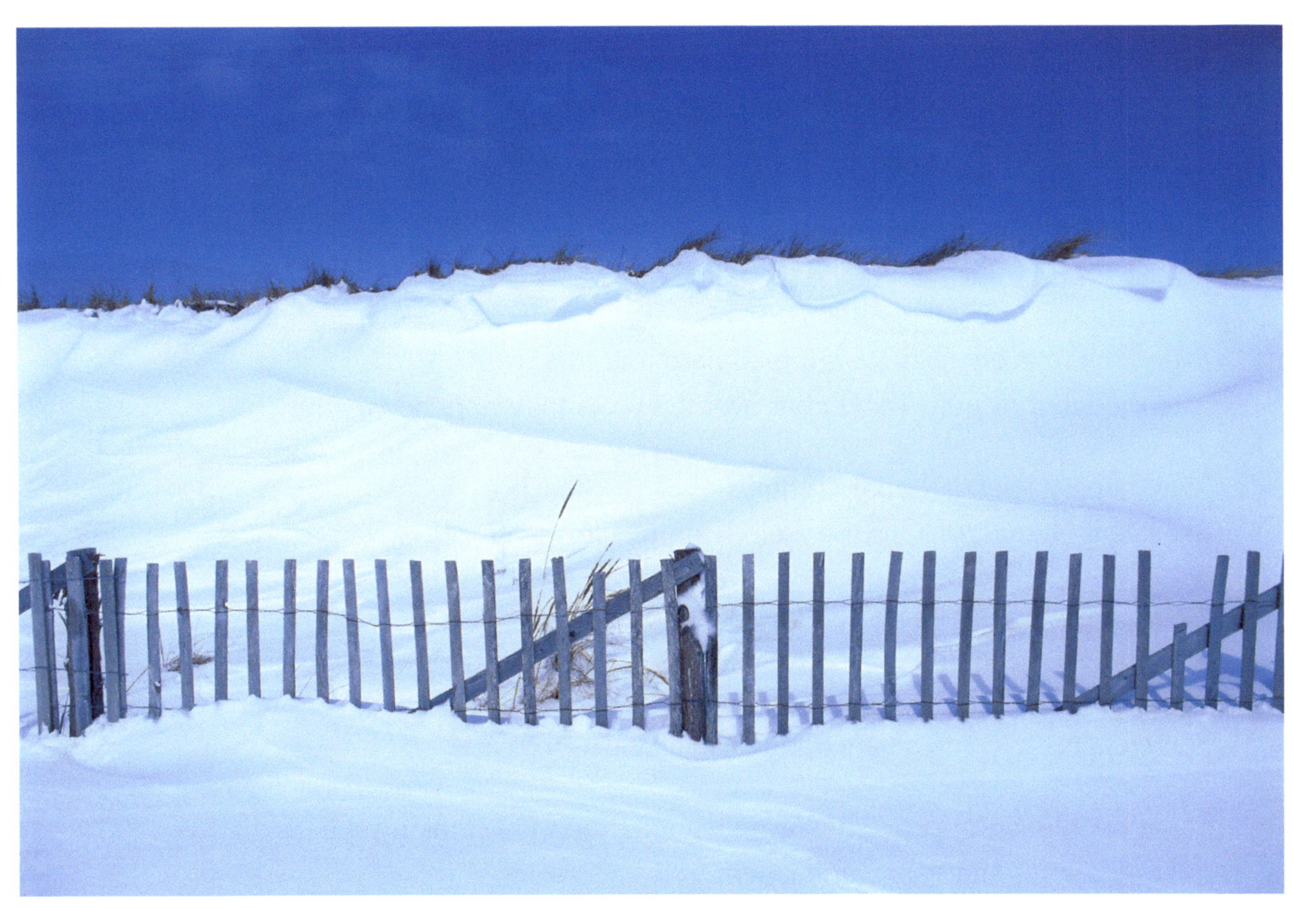

The Fourth Chain

Three of his chains were longer than most.
The first, each link forged from the years walking this earth.
The second, each link forged from a lifetime of memories created.
The third, each link forged from the scores of lives he affected.

The fourth chain, forged from sins and regrets,
was as short as any man could hope for.

Every link in every chain was forged hard and true.
And though they grew in number over the years they bore no weight.

They hung suspended from his limbs
like silent chimes, playing the melody of his life.

As he forged ahead he carried them with pride
of a life well lived, full of determination and purpose.

Some chains become an anchor that shackles us in place.

Some people live at peace, unaware yet tethered to a shrinking sphere,
their memories fading in waning light.

Others struggle and strain against the sins and regrets
that squeeze and strangle and suffocate.

Yet for a soul so inquisitive and shining bright,
it was the anchor of age that became the unbearable burden.

And so, he sought release from an earth-bound angel.

And as his body is covered in a shroud of white,
he soars above us unbound.

But for those of us left behind,
we stare down at the fourth chain at our feet,
and we carry the links of our choosing.

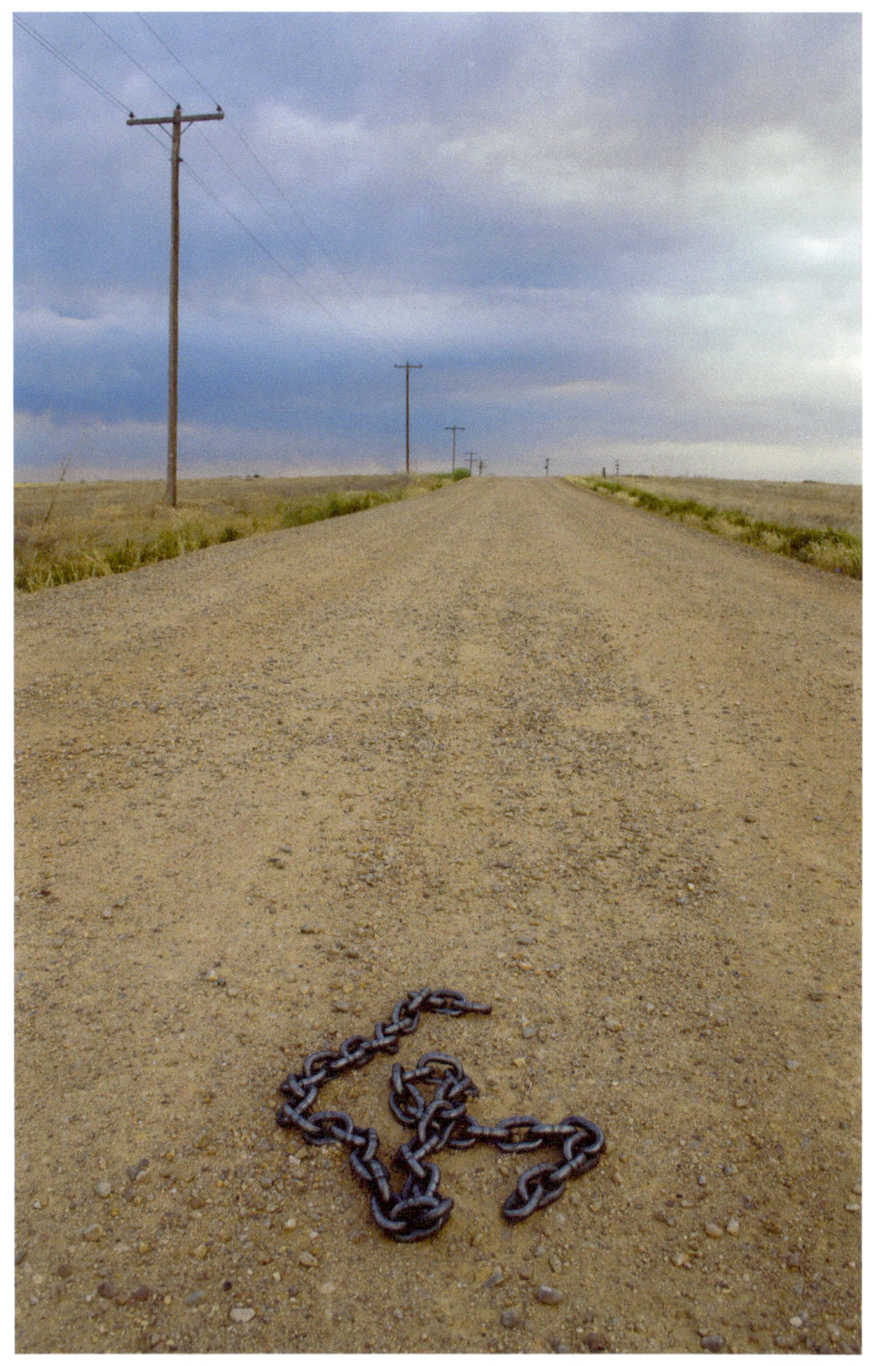

The Girl Beside the Car

On the top shelf in the closet I find beautiful pastel drawings of flowers,
pen and ink illustrations of Grand Central Station,
and watercolors of flowing gowns of her own design.

They were created when there was time to do such things,
before the need for a paycheck,
and before the need to care for us all.

Regrets wash in like the tide.
I should have talked to her more.

Shelley and Keats and Browning and Dickenson
hold their respected places on the bookshelf.
I should have talked to her more.

All those holiday visits, I relaxed by the fire, while she was in the kitchen.
She was doing what she wanted to do.
And I was doing what she wanted me to do.
But I wish I had talked to her more.

Photos come down from the walls,
leaving hooks and faded, dusty outlines,
and the house begins to feel like a Whoville house on Christmas morning,
except the Grinch can never return what was taken.

Sounds from the highway drift in, from up the hill.
It's hard to dismantle her life.
A life built brick by brick, year after year, with the idea of creating a home.
The home is now merely an empty shell, as is her body lying in the casket.

I'll leave carrying what memories and mementos I can.
The rest will be scattered to the winds, as soon her ashes will be.

Still, there is the sound of the road.
It haunts me in the early morning hours,
stirring memories of all the pre-dawn departures,
saying goodbye to the people I love.

She's just a young girl in the old black and white photo.
She's standing beside her father's car,
her hair wet, wearing a bathing suit, a towel around her neck.
She had been swimming, up at the lake.

Despite all the good memories I cling to,
this is often how I like to picture her,
before life got hard,
before the sacrifices for our benefit,
before cancer and the other ailments of age.

She's smiling the innocent, carefree smile of youth, that says,
right here, right now, there's nowhere else I'd rather be.
"Today is perfect," says the girl beside the car.

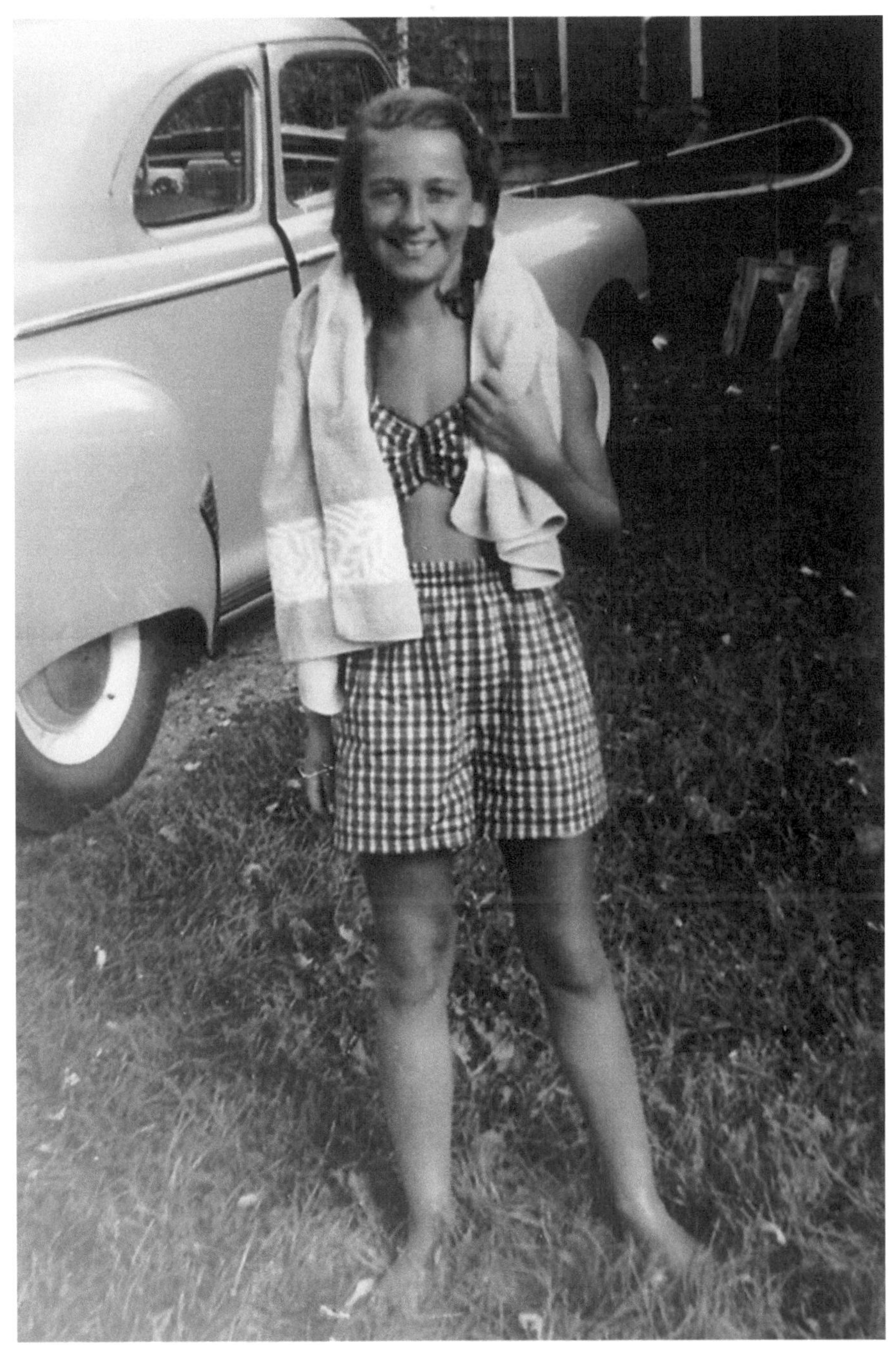

Chairs of Stone

In a dream I gaze down upon
a flat-topped sandstone mesa,
an island of rock perched
above a desert of blue.

Two worn chairs of stone
sit side by side on top of the mesa,
facing the sea,
waiting for the lovers to return.

A lovely young girl,
her vision as clear as day,
appears like a movie on the water,
the sea smooth as glass.

She plays their song on a violin,
joyfully,
waiting for the lovers to return
from the sea.

I wait out the day,
and into the night,
hoping to see the silvery moonlight
play over their mesa in the sky.

But the island is moving away from land,
and a storm is brewing.

I never see
the lovers return
to their thrones on the mesa,
perched above the desert of blue.

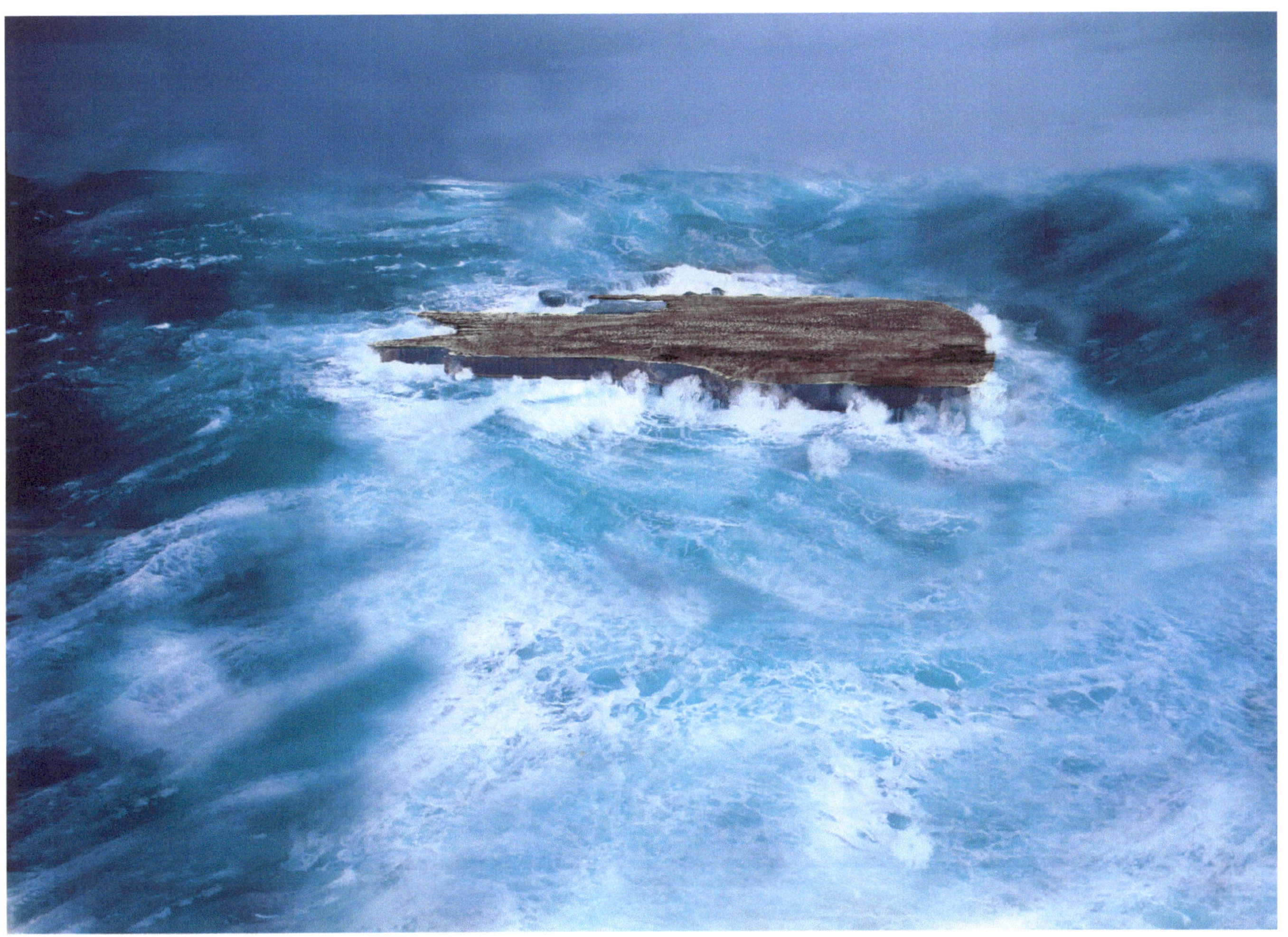

Chalk White

Before,
the poet thought often about harnessing a pen,
but the time to sit and ponder eluded him.

His journal was like a blackboard
in a dark school room,
under the long summer sun.

It had been turn after turn of the earth
since she was gone.

How fortunate he was now
to be unencumbered from all the daily minutia
that previously had consumed his days.

After,
he stared at the chalk white page,
but it just stared back.

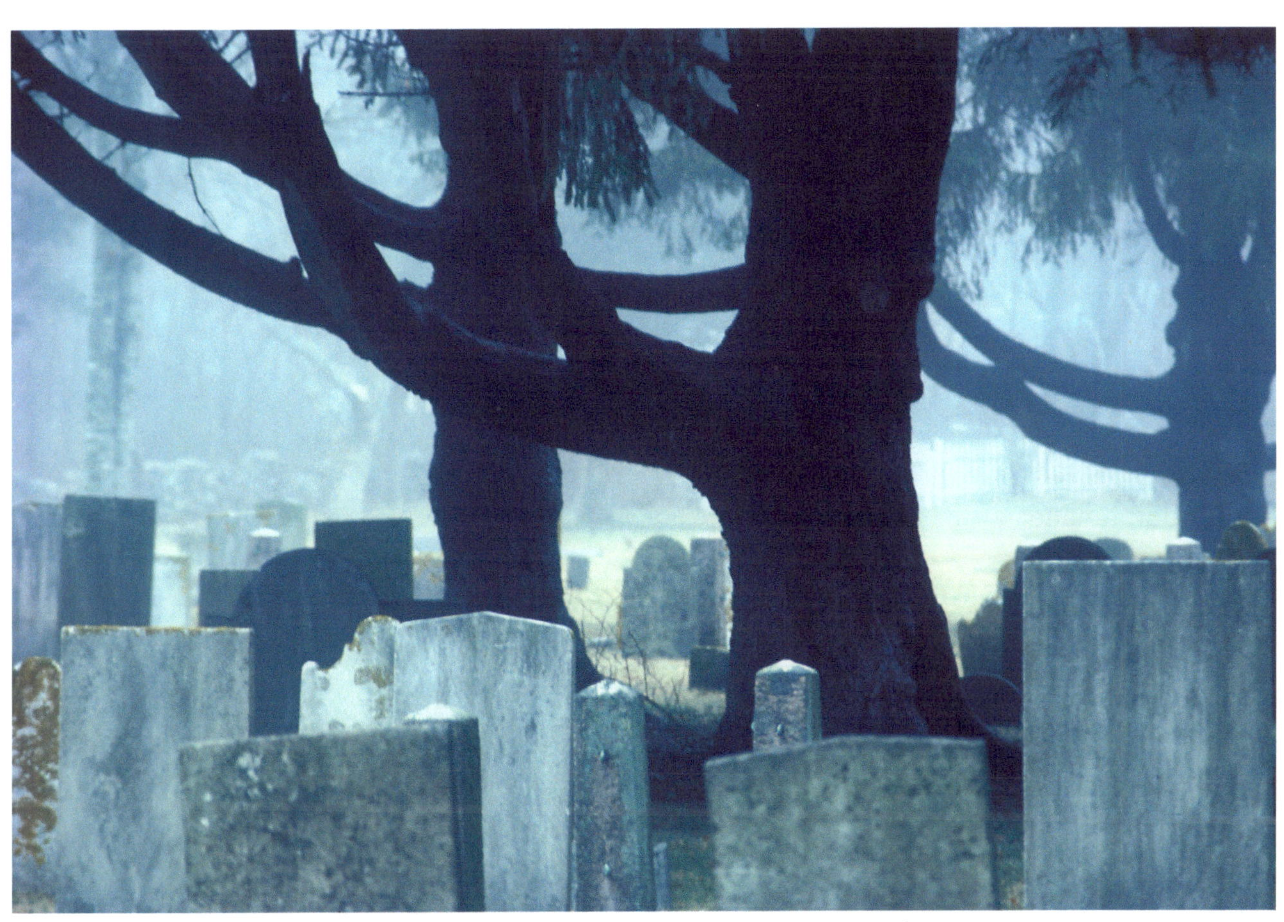

The Edge

She left me standin' in gravel and dust
As her tires, they kicked up at me
It wasn't no surprise to anyone
Least of all to me

I can't undo the things I've done
Even staring down the barrel of a blue steel gun
That's why every rise of that burnin' sun
Finds me once again on a stone cold run

Heads or tails
It don't matter what I choose
Heads or tails
It don't matter what I choose
I'm always on the edge
So either way I lose

I didn't ever have a daddy
Ain't never gonna have a son
So these blessed sins I carry
Gonna be mine until I'm done

Now these sins I carry, they're a heavy load
Ain't much company, on a long empty road
Can't move forward, I'm caught in a trap
Ain't no way she'd ever take me back

Heads or tails
It don't matter what I choose
Heads or tails
It don't matter what I choose
I'm always on the edge
So either way I lose

All you angels of mercy
Won't you please come lift me up?
'Cause I've got more than I can handle
And I've just about had enough

All you angels of mercy
Won't you please come lift me up?
'Cause my past won't let me go, Lord
And I've just about given up

All you angels of mercy
I know there's a heavy price to pay
All you angels of mercy
Please come down and take me away

Heads or tails
It don't matter what I choose
Heads or tails
It don't matter what I choose
I'm always on the edge
So either way I lose

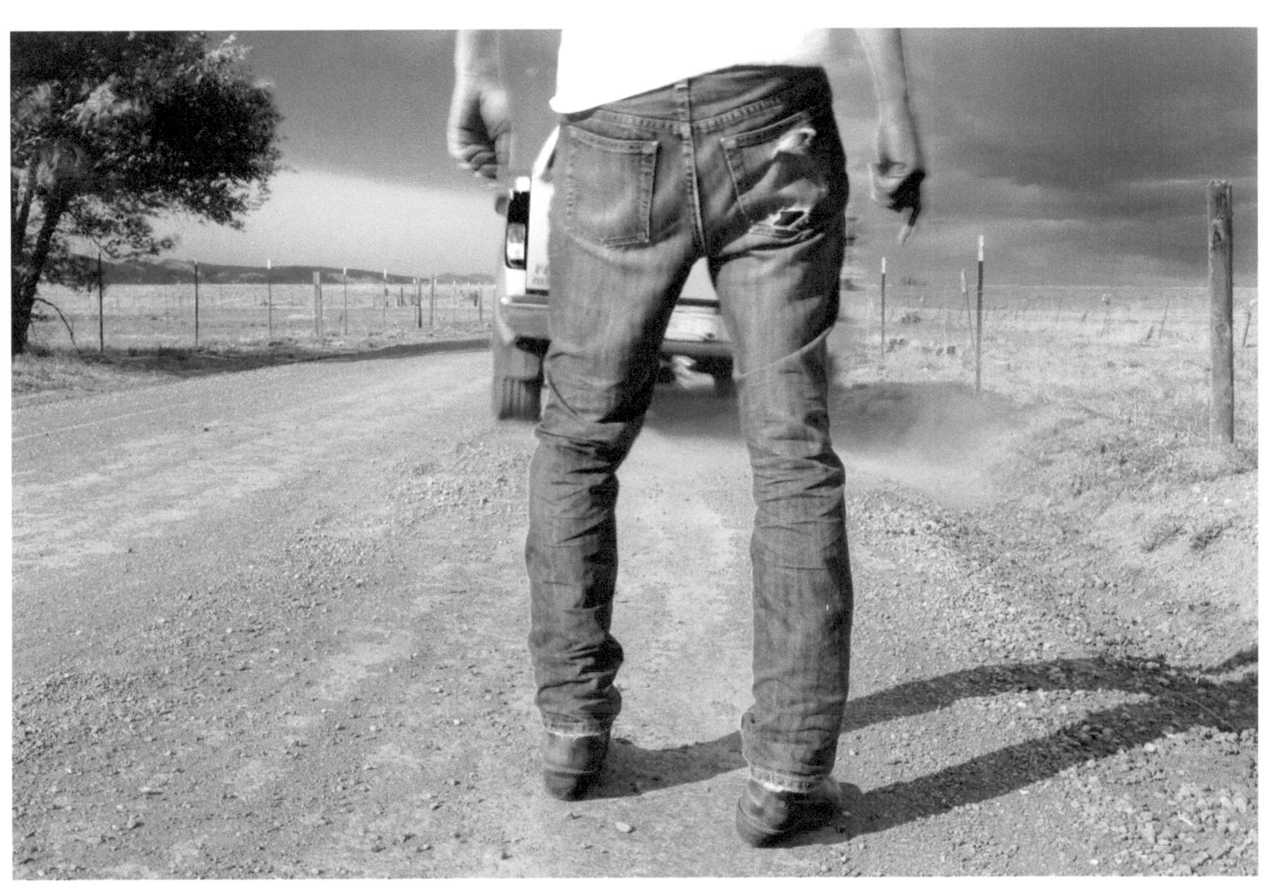

The Bridge

I have to tell you something
I heard your song today
But your unfinished lyrics,
They hang precariously out in space

Your voice was still and silent
Though you hoped someone would hear
Your voice was full of music
Lying hidden and concealed

I understand a little
Of what it was that brought you here
If only I had known enough
To whisper in your ear

Your song remains unfinished
With many verses yet to write
I hope you rise tomorrow
Just make it through the night

I have to tell you something
As you're standing on the bridge
I really like your song
And I want you to live

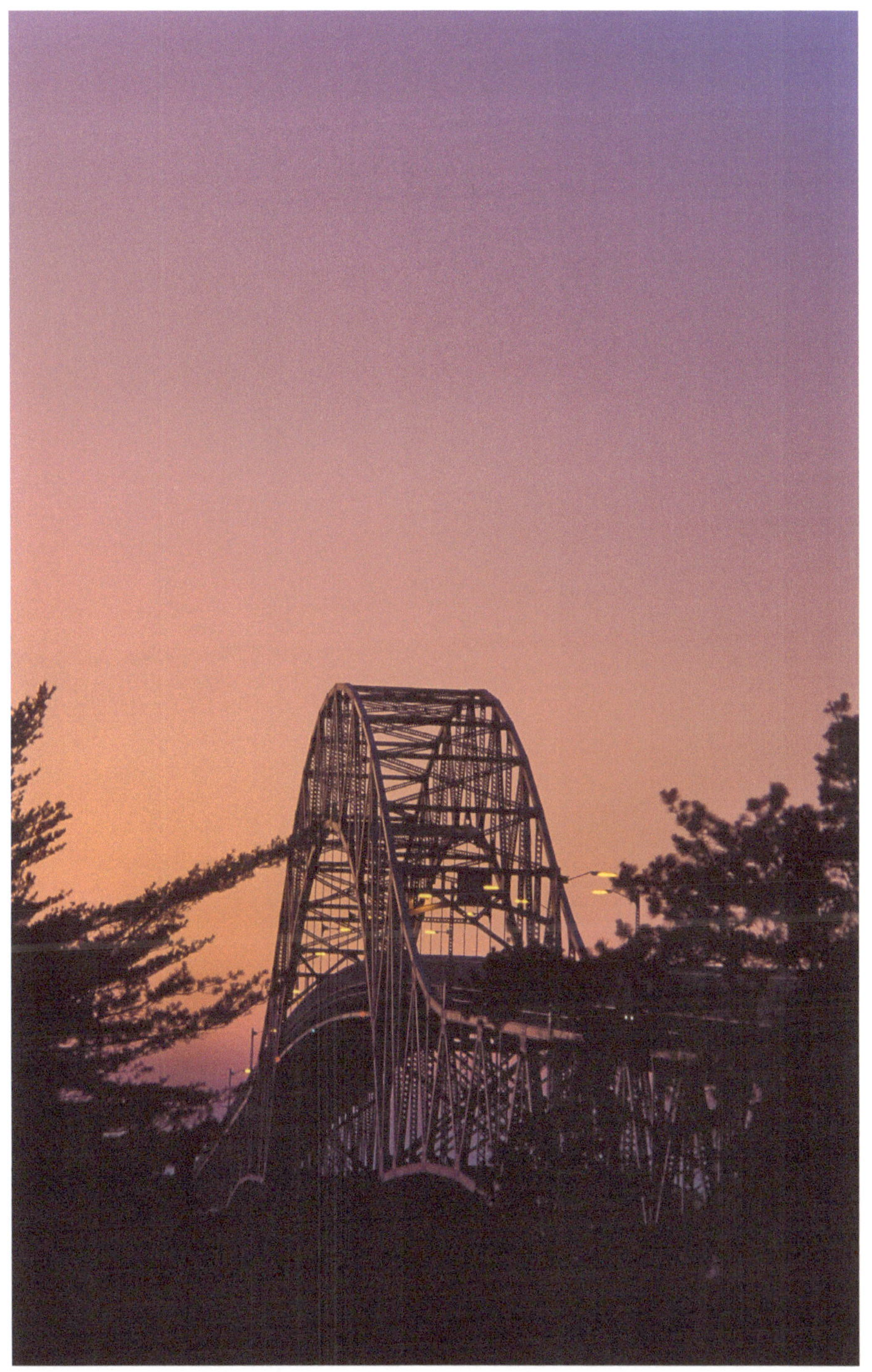

My Own Worst Enemy

He tells me I'm no good.
He tells me I'm not a good husband,
or father,
or brother,
or son.
He tells me that I could have been more generous,
more giving,
more patient,
more understanding,
more sympathetic.
He tells me that I have accomplished little, in these many long years.

So I pull on my woolen coat,
draw up the high collar,
and go for a walk in the winter fields.

The open blue sky tells me that the world is still full of possibilities.
The few remaining crinkled oak leaves click together,
and shoots of browned grasses sticking up through the settled snow wave at me,
telling me there is still more time.

The geese flying south call out to me,
telling me there is warmth just around the corner.
A few of the weary travelers land, and rest, on the frozen ring of my pond,
standing on one webbed foot, and then the other,
telling me that I can survive the cold simply by changing my position.
The snow crunches and squeaks under foot,
and it tells me that the world is a better place with me in it.

I pause in my tracks,
and the winter quiet is enough to still him,
though even now he strains to be heard.

I exhale him out,
and I watch him slowly dissipate
into the chill December air.

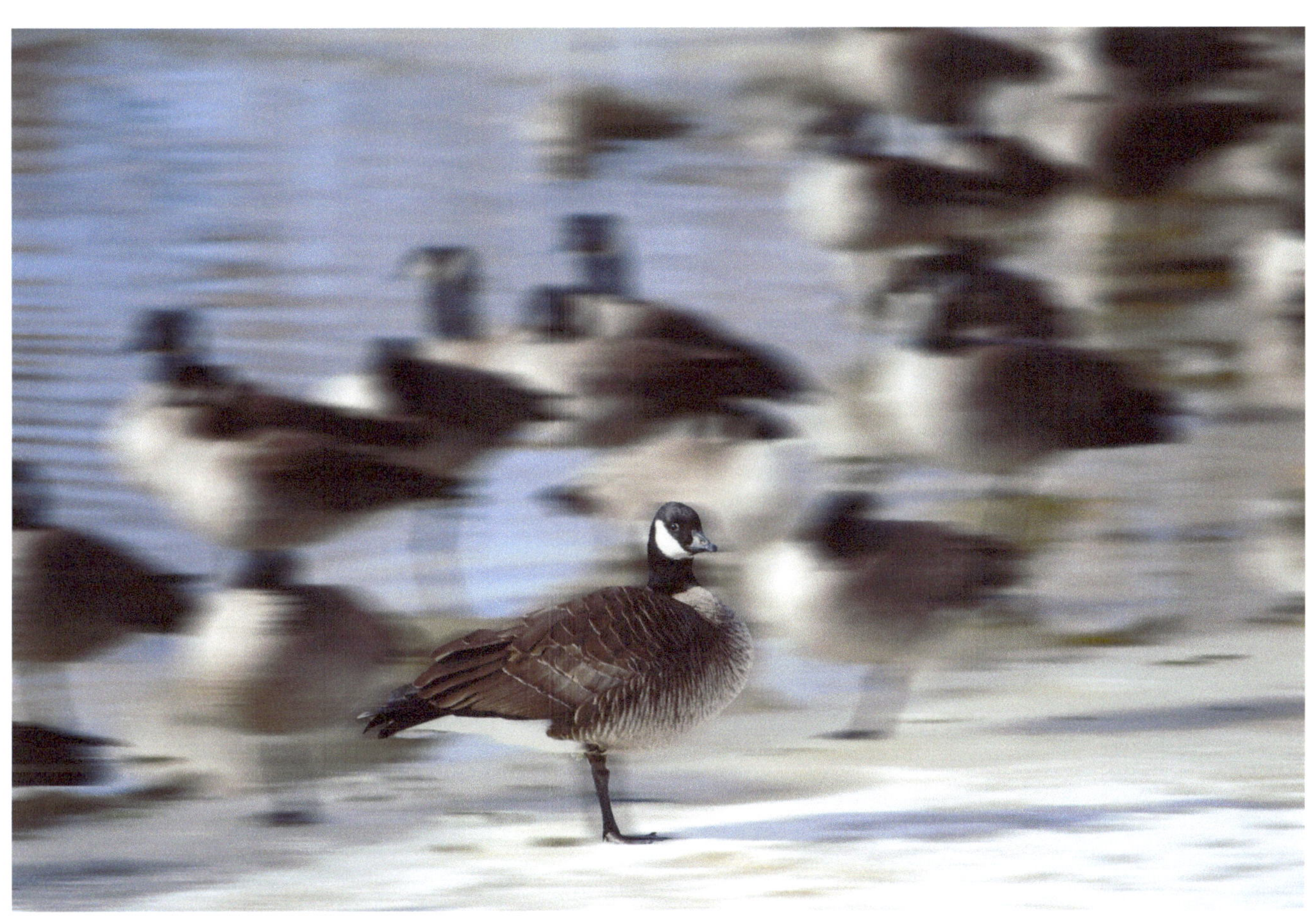

Chapter 3 - Evolution

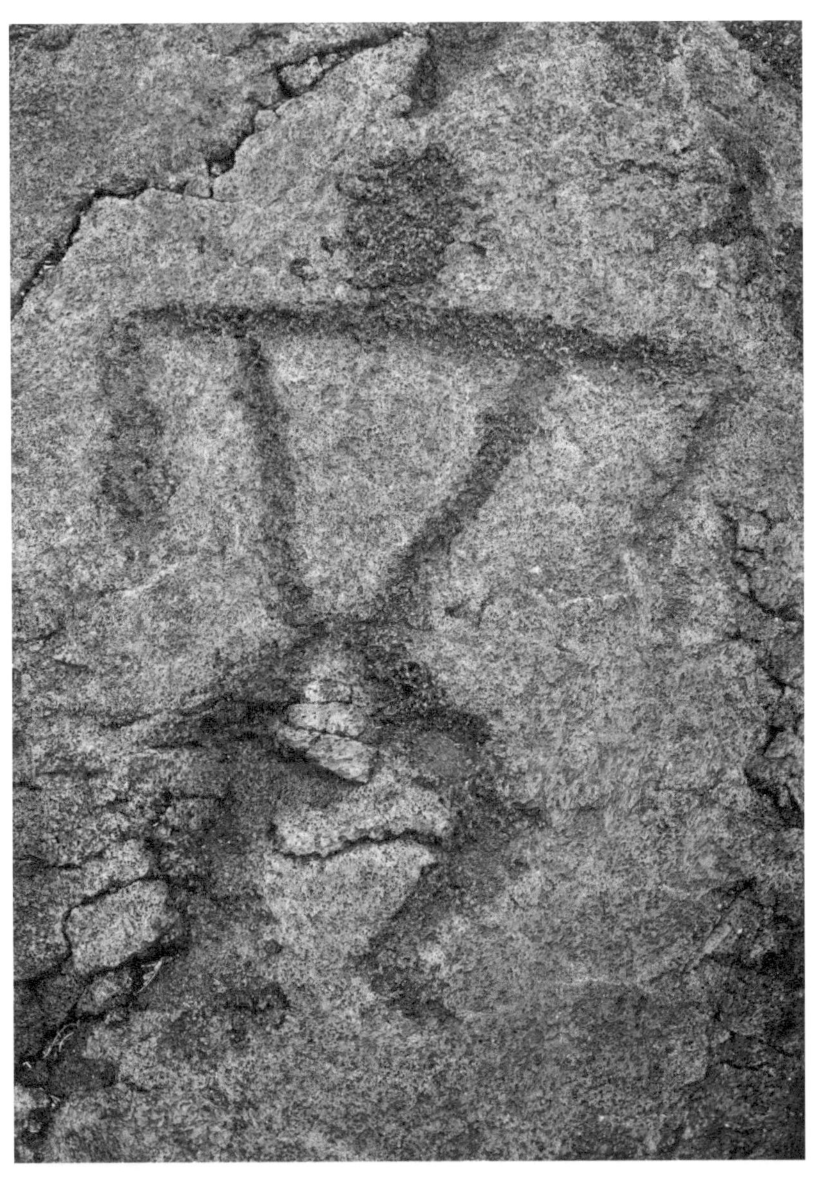

Sanctuary

The monks found sanctuary on Skellig Michael,
off the jagged coast of the Emerald Isle.
They had fled a feud with the Kings of Cashel,
and carved life and prayer out of the island in the sky.

Their numbers 'ere but a dozen or so,
they built dry, beehive cells.
Shelter from the gales of the North Atlantic
that battered them, truth do tell.

Four hundred years and more
did they sustain their souls,
until Viking invasions shattered their peace,
and forced them from their knolls.

The puffins and shearwaters of Skellig Michael
find sanctuary underground,
safe from the black-backed and herring gulls
that on the winds abound.

The seals of Great Blasket found sanctuary
only after the humans departed.
Free from the threat of the hunt, they now
bask on the beach, unguarded.

Legend holds that men in their currach,
rowing home to the Blasket Islands,
heard music rise through the skin of their boat,
unknown to those of Ireland.

The musician among them, that night by oil light,
penned the Song of the Fairies,
in reverence to the whale song they heard on that day,
that the winds did mysteriously carry.

All good men, the fishermen swore on a cross
that in those waters, whales should not be.
Why did they grace those souls that day?
Perhaps they sought sanctuary.

And the monk and the puffin and the whale sang,
as if all children of earth.
Where can we lay our heads to rest,
and who will know our worth?

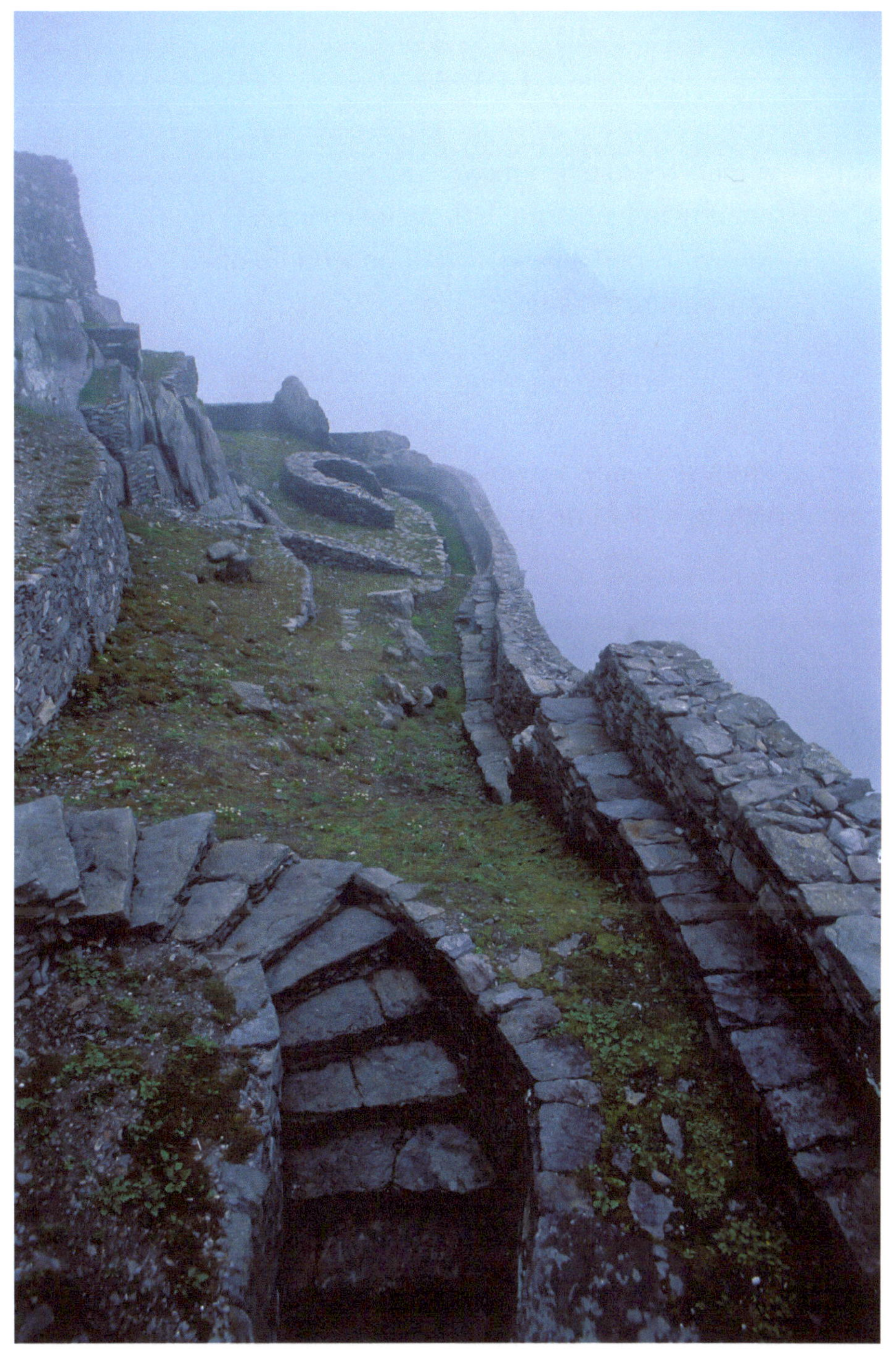

Lines

A man approached me,
offering to work for a little spare change.
Knowing, perhaps, that I had no work to offer,
was I being fed a line?

We are fed line after line,
as if starving for what we hope to hear.
Promises made are not promises kept.
Where is our line in the sand?

Where is our line in the sand,
when the starving go hungry,
the uninsured die,
and liars get rich?

The Nazca lines in the desert sands of Peru
suggest that earth has been visited before.
But are these lines a path to our past,
or to our future?

The lines in the mirror
suggest an evolution of sorts.
I only hope that in time my heart will soar,
and I can look at the lines with peace.

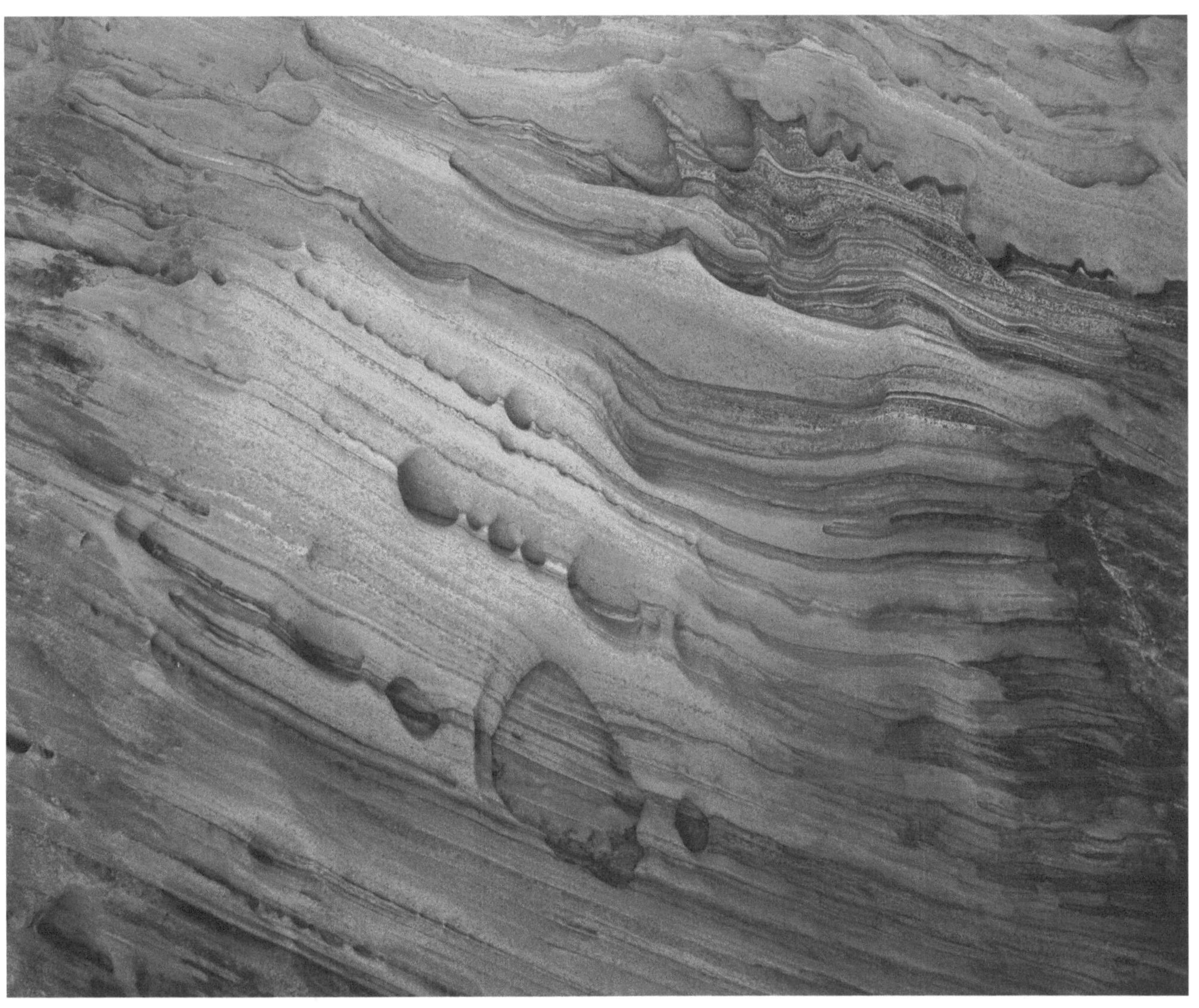

The Fallen

There has been a war.
In the land of ancient giants, the warriors hide the front lines from view.
Yet the evidence is clear, as loud lumbering monsters thunder by,
the fallen stripped of their limbs and stacked in mobile mass graves.

On the field of battle, the slaughter is without mercy.
The victims, cut off at their knees and ankles, do not litter the arena.
No prisoners taken, no women or children spared.
We are all collateral damage.

From the air, the battleground is a patchwork,
a sickening quilt of devastation.
The selective extraction is a vision of politics and greed,
shock and awe at the loss of the treasured.

The war continues, I fear victory is certain.
Rejuvenation of the vanquished is too slow.
Adaptation and migration are not viable routes of escape.
Scars in the land, and scars in my heart.

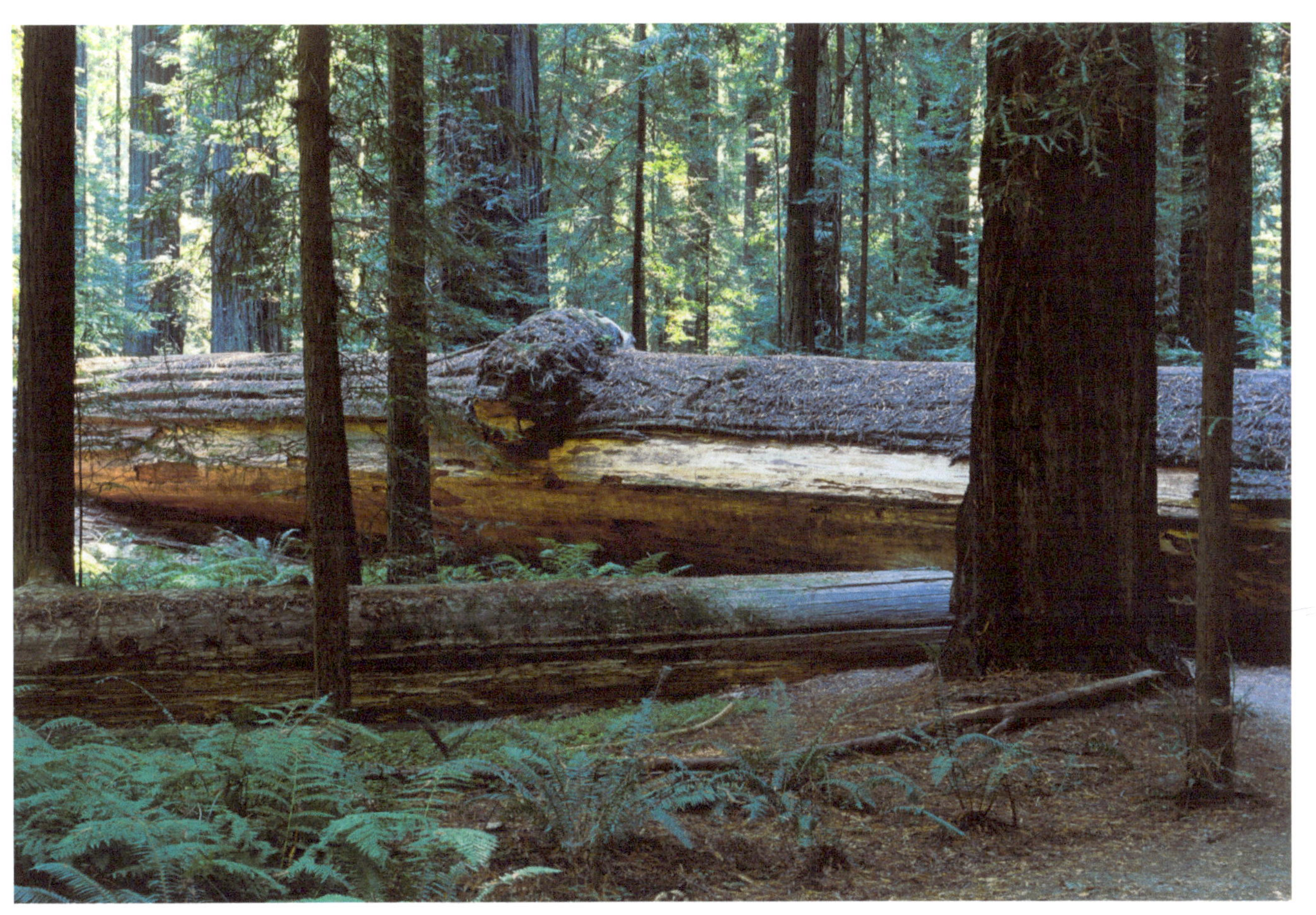

When the Dinosaurs Roamed

Sitting on the bank of the Green River,
cottonwood leaves clicking in the warm wind,
I stare up at the massive rift in Split Mountain,
where the river found a weak spot in the earth
and down cut between the red-colored Morgan
and buff-colored Weber formations,
leaving fantastic canyons, hoodoos, and spires.

A deer forages on low green shrubs up the sandy bank,
and a Bierstadt sky takes on painterly color
as the sun falls slowly in the west.
Tall cumulonimbus clouds are pure white at their peak,
transitioning to a brooding gray middle
and a fiery red base, lit up from below.
A little south, virga rain falls in a misty gray watercolor wash,
never reaching the dry desert ground.

It's hard to imagine back 150 million years,
when the land was flat savannah,
when the continent was further south,
when dinosaurs roamed the land.

Camarasaurus and stegosaurus
ruled this land until a drought killed them off.
A catastrophic flood later piled up and buried their bones,
hidden until 1909.

A cosmic collision ended much of the rest of life
in the 5th great mass extinction,
making room for new branches
in the tree of evolution.

Humans only came to be
a mere minute and seventeen seconds ago,
if earth's history was a day.

In less than a second, we've started the 6th mass extinction.

As my Bierstadt sunset fades to night,
a billion stars are revealed.
I know I can't see it, but somewhere there is light,
traveling through the ether,
having set out on its path
when the dinosaurs roamed.

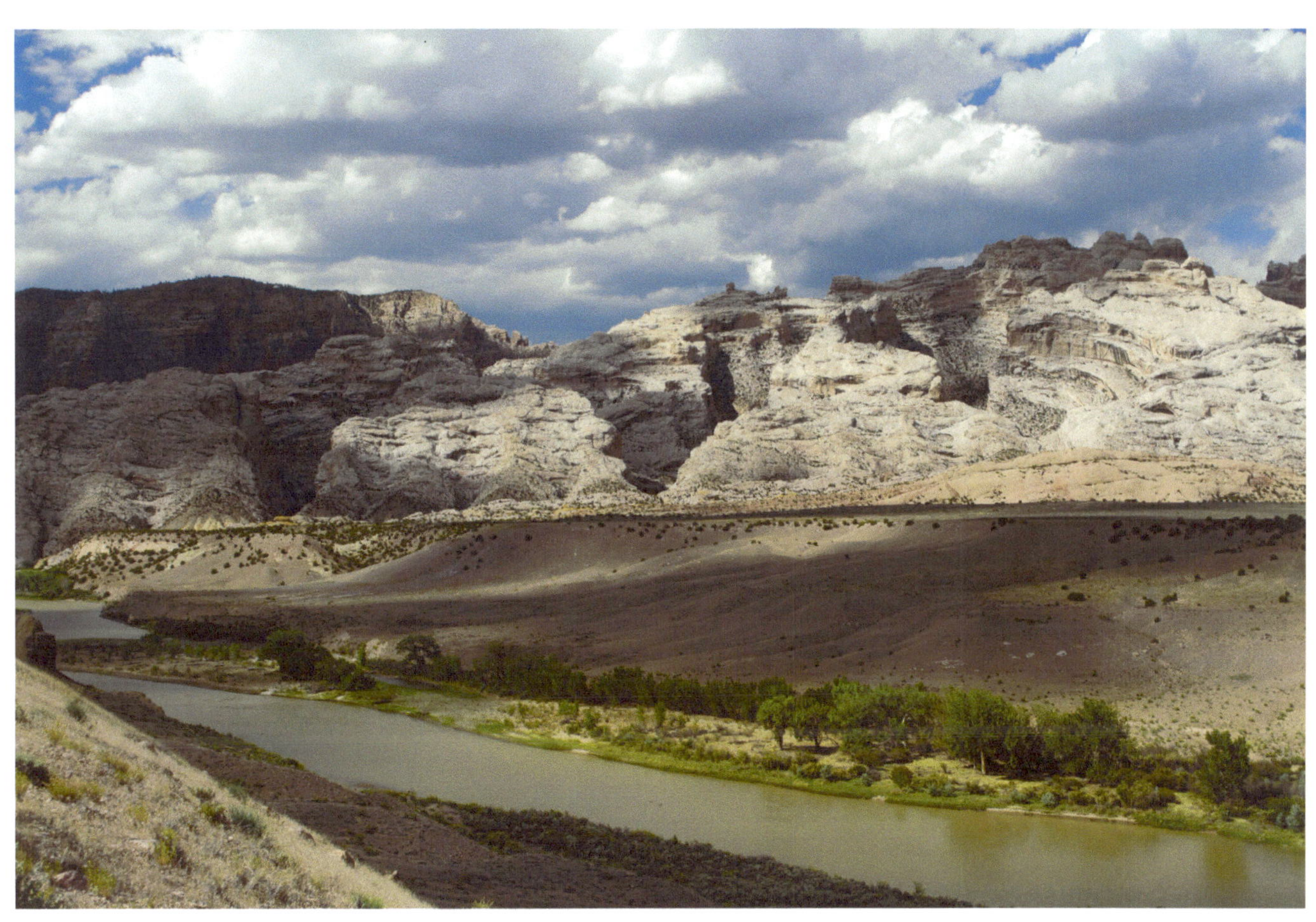

The Wolf at the Door

Inspired by a true story...

I heard a strange knocking.
Strange, not for the hour,
as the sun was up.

Well, not so much the sun
as a gray light creeping through
the late December sky.

No, it was strange because
we don't get many visitors out here
this time of year,

a two-mile walk or ski in from the road,
set apart as we are up here
in the great north woods.

Strange, too, for the sound
of the knocking.
Soft enough that I almost didn't catch it,
save for the quiet that enveloped
the cabin like a woolen blanket.

And there was a pause between
the solitary knocks,
a number of seconds apart,
like an old grandfather clock that
hadn't been wound in quite some time.

I left the kitchen and entered
the living room,
where I saw him,
standing there alone,
at the big window that stares
out over the open field,
an ancient bog in summer
that now lies buried
beneath feet of cold snow.

He was dark as night,
and dusted with ice crystal stars.
Set against a sea of white,
he looked like a weathered old black and white photograph,
preserved in time.

His slow breaths came out
as cold smoke,
and a huge paw came up and
gently thumped against the glass,
holding it there, and pausing
before it slid down to the ground.
His yellow eyes met my blues.

"June," I said.
She and the boys came in,
then stopped short with a hushed gasp.
"He wants to come in," I said.

We had heard the pack howl
on rare occasions.
The last time was late at night
under the cool light of a blood-red harvest moon.

And I had seen them, once,
taking down a sick or injured fawn,
in the deep, snowy wood.

I looked at June,
and then the boys,
and then glanced towards
the back of the cabin.
She ushered them gently back into the den.

I opened the door slowly,
and he looked at me,
pausing on the threshold.

A cold blast hit my face as a warm blast hit his.

And on those big paws,
he softly padded past me,
across the room,
and gingerly laid down on the
warm stone hearth
next to the wood stove.

I sat with him,
and stroked my grizzled beard.
And as the ice crystals began to melt
on his grizzled fur,
I put my hand on his chest.

I could feel his heart beating, slow.

And his yellow eyes met my blues,
and he asked me if he could stay,
just a little while longer.

The pine sap popped
behind the soot-covered, smoky glass,
and he was so close to the stove
I thought his fur would singe.
I guess he just wanted to feel
the warmth in his old bones
one last time.

Generation upon generation
of adaptation and survival
can't keep the wolf from the door.

And the light finally left
those golden eyes,
and his chest sank a little
closer to the ground.

And we kept him
in the old ice shack
until spring came,
and the ground thawed.

And we buried him
in a grove of paper birch
out behind the cabin,
bathed in golden light.

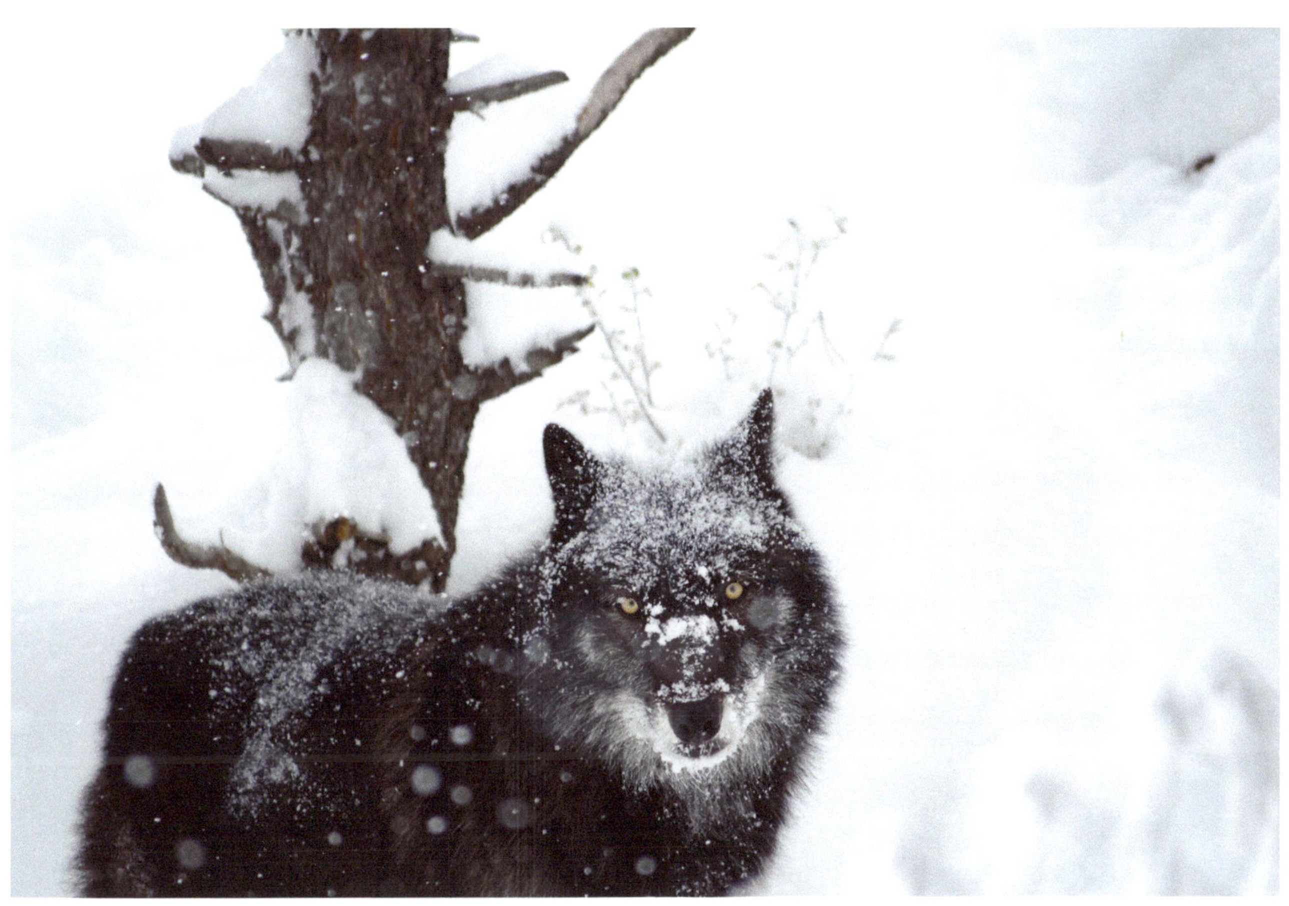

R/Evolutions

In the central Ethiopian Highlands,
gelada monkeys make their morning ascent
from their safe sleeping haven on cliffs at 11,000 feet,
much as they have done for thousands of years.

Known as "bleeding hearts" for the red chest patches that change color
when the mood is right, the geladas are guarded by soldiers slinging Kalashnikovs.
An exploding population, the need for crop and grazing land, and climate change
are all conspiring to test the geladas and their guardians.

It is a race against time for the Yupiks of Quinhagak,
on the southwest coast of Alaska.
Thawing permafrost and rising seas threaten to unearth
and destroy ancestral artifacts that had been frozen in time.

An intact uluaq is retrieved before the storm.
Viewed from one side,
the cutting tool handle looks like a whale.
From the other side, a seal.

This mask is a walrus, but it is also a person.
This box is a kayak, but also a seal.
They are symbols of the Yupik belief that everything
is in a constant state of transformation.

With weathered eyes,
they watch language and culture erode
as quickly as the shoreline.
They know that survival requires adaptation.

With instinctual eyes,
the geladas gaze down over the Great Rift Valley,
where bone diggers found Lucy,
one of the mothers of human evolution.

Three million years old, she was named after
"Lucy in the Sky with Diamonds,"
The Beatles song scientists played repeatedly
during the celebration of her discovery.

We have *evolved* a great deal since Lucy,
while roaming this living earth.
Andeans and Tibetans adapted to high altitudes.
Aboriginals adapted to desert extremes.
But still we roam in uncharted territory.

A Spaniard was the first to be labeled a Cyborg.
With a chip in his head,
and an antenna protruding out,
he sees "color" in ways we do not.

What does it mean
when we can buy eye color,
or skin color,
or the smartest embryo?
Can we engineer survival of the fittest?

The earth revolves upon its axis,
and revolves around the sun,
both at near constant rates
set long ago by heavenly forces.

Yet earth itself,
and we resident humans,
are *evolving* at breakneck speed.
Can either survive the coming revolution?

In the Central African Republic,
a thousand miles from the geladas,
a farmer walks his dusty furrows,
collecting colorful butterfly wings
that have settled in his fields.

He transforms them into works of art,
creating wondrous scenes of life in his homeland.
They appear as though made of stained glass,
as beautiful as in any cathedral.

In his war-torn country,
his view through the looking glass of his art
helps him heal,
and helps him remember
peacefulness of the past.

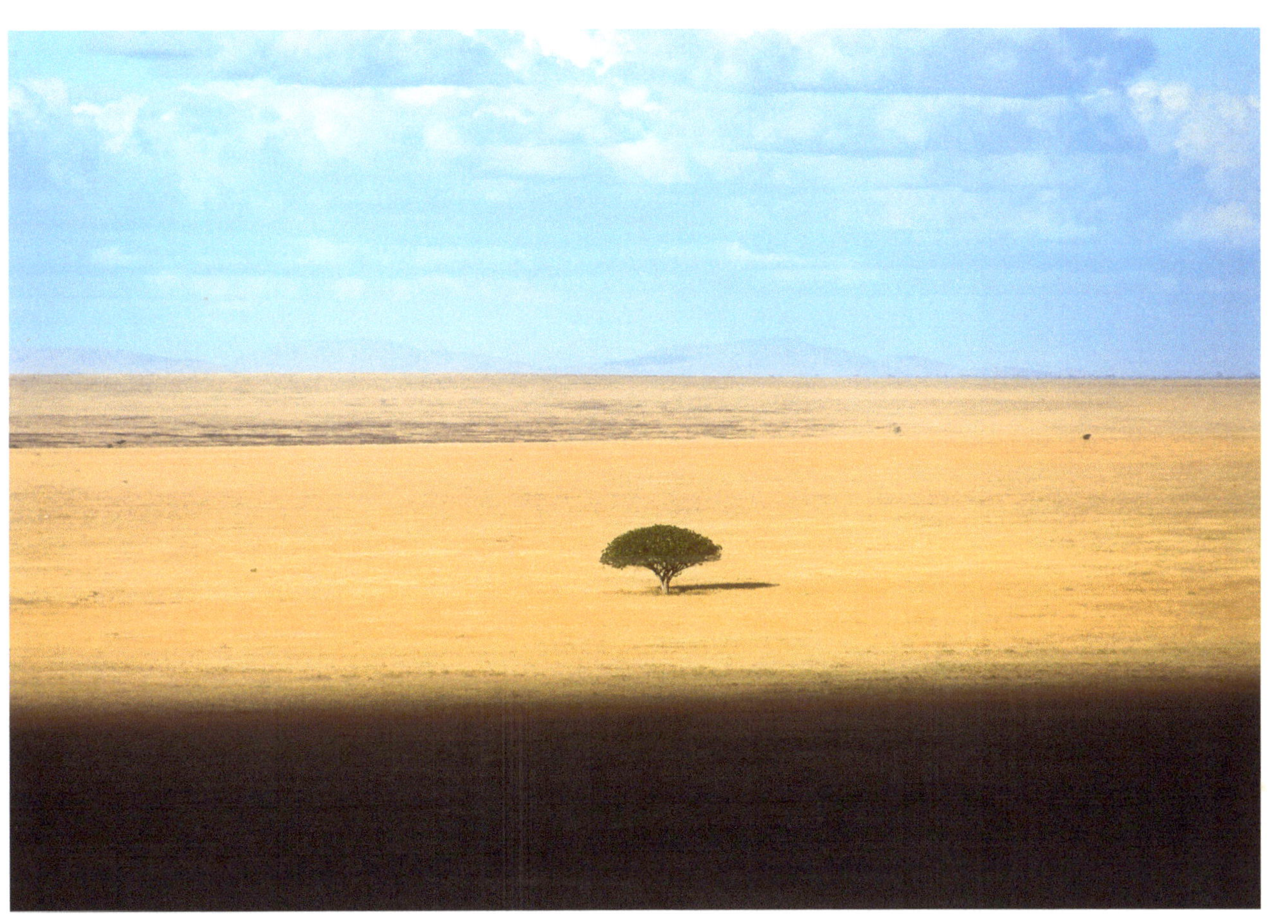

Chapter 4 - Beauty

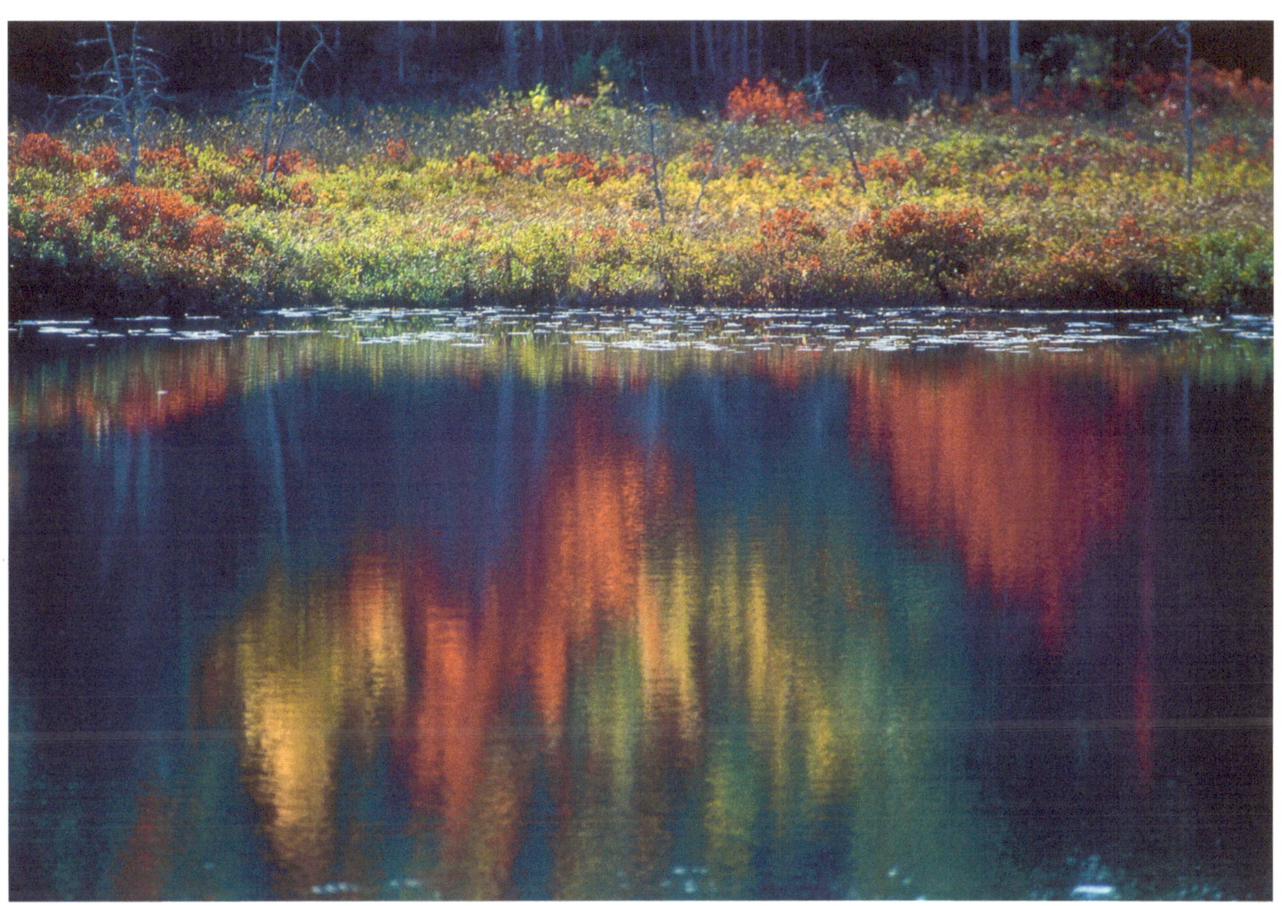

Inception

In the summertime snow of cottonwood seeds,
I sit on the bank of a small creek and watch
as their ballet of choreographed descent on the breeze ends,
and they are whisked away in the ripping current.

The rushing water mesmerizes me.
Smooth and silent, there is a clear reach
of laminar flow that cascades
over a granite boulder, creating a maelstrom
of froth and foam, amid a constant roar.

Eventually, I break my gaze
and raise my eyes towards the far bank,
which briefly seems to move upstream
in a perception-bending, inception-like moment.

Five brightly colored mallards, males,
slowly paddle the opposite shore, out of the fast flow.
They seem to spend half their time preening,
and half their time prodding the shallow muck
for tasty bits of vegetation.

Upstream, a graceful blue heron
deftly patrols the shallows
in search of fish to be snatched
with its long beak.

Downstream, a fly fisherman
slowly works the pools and riffles,
in search of fish to be snatched
with his barbed hook.

What have I done, to deserve living
in the shadow of the Rockies,
with snow-capped peaks
piercing through pure azure skies,
and glistening streams,
and rugged mountain trails,
and graceful hawks souring on thermals?

What have I done,
while others suffer the slings and arrows
of outrageous misfortune?

What have I done to deserve this beautiful life?

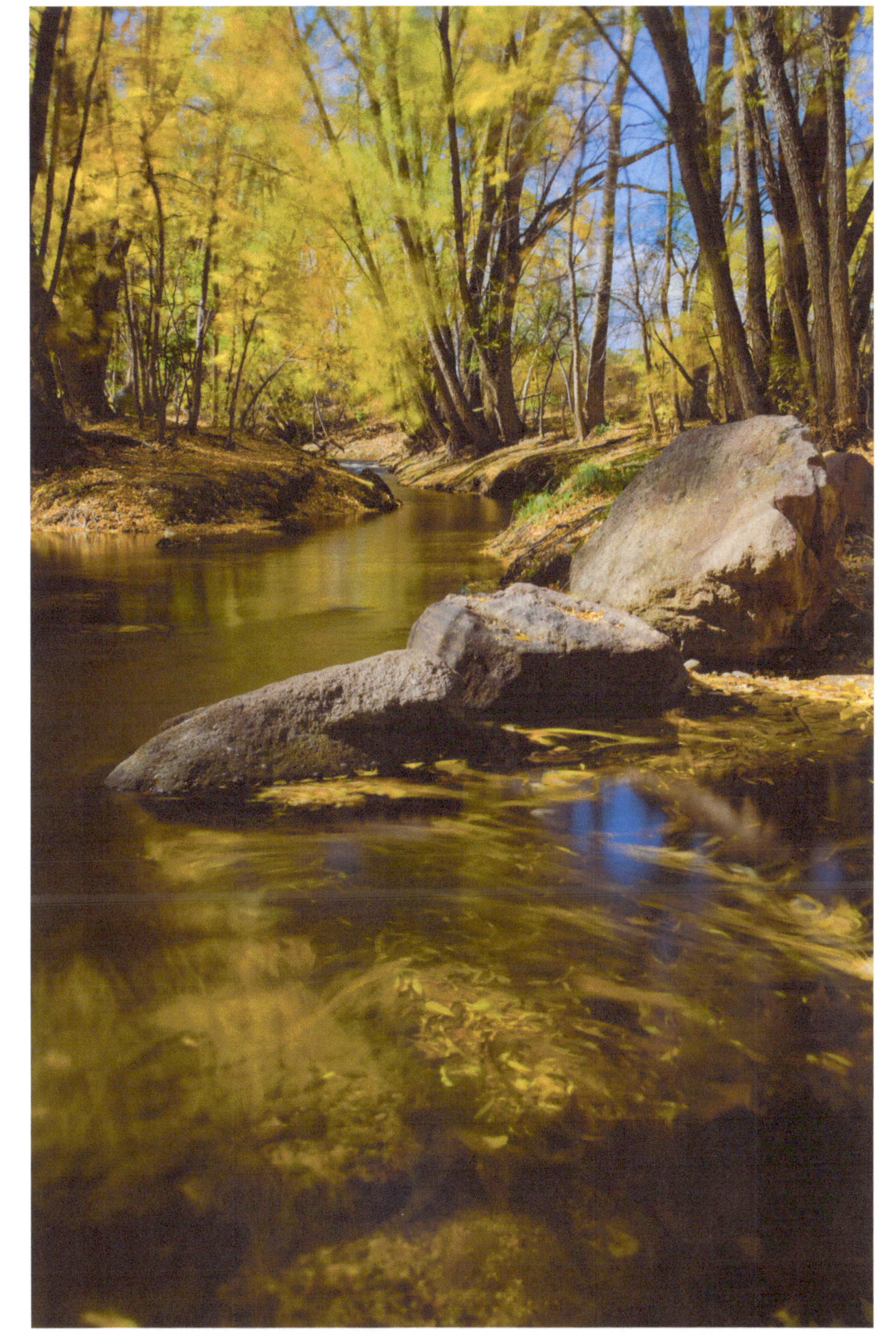

Color

I've never been in the back seat of a black and white.
I've never seen the muzzle of a gun pointed at my face,
either with or without cause.

What little I know is from black and white print,
but even therein whatever truth may lie
seems more like shades of gray.

Azure skies sweep overhead,
while cerulean seas rise and fall like breath across the globe.
Tawny grasslands shimmer across the western prairie
under wide open skies,
and jade jungles blanket the humid tropics.
I am awed by the color that surrounds us.

They say a black and white photo is timeless,
but color makes our world unique.
Philae landed on Churyumov–Gerasimenko,
a lifeless comet hurtling through infinite space.
But the pictures it sent back just confirmed for me
that most of the universe is just dark matter.

We live on a brilliant blue orb, full of life and color.
Have you ever seen the iridescent mandarin fish,
the pastel-hued dwarf kingfisher,
or the glowing blue morpho butterfly?
I am awed by the color that surrounds us.

Of Shimmering Skies and Gentle Seas

On a chilled autumn night camped out high in the Rockies,
tucked down into the warmth of my bag,
and serenaded by the sounds of a clear cascade,
I couldn't help but gaze upon
the ghostly crescent hull of the moon,
slicing quietly through the inky black sea above me,
its wake sending out ripples
that triggered the phosphorescence
of countless sparkling stars,
precious gems
in the constellations of creation.

I was reminded of a quiet spring night
down Bermuda way,
where I heard humpbacks sing
as they passed silently beneath our ship,
their mournful melody brought to my ears
by a hydrophone hanging off the stern.

On that particular night,
the phosphorescence of the stars
was mirrored by the bioluminescence in our wake,
the ship's hull bathed in eerie blue light,
as we gently rose and then fell on a low southerly swell.

Thinking back upon the ancient mariners,
I excused them for believing the earth
was the center of all things,
that as the milky way soared overhead on zephyr winds,
the heavens must revolve around us.
Oh, what they must have thought of shooting stars!

But just as the crescent moon sinks beneath
the Sangre de Cristos,
and leviathans swim hidden
on their long migration home,
we would do well to remember that we
are merely passing through,
and we would do well to cherish moonlit nights
of shimmering skies and gentle seas.

Provo Palette

On the island of Providenciales,
where ripsaw music carries on fair winds and tides,
there are more shades of blue and green
than Eskimo words for snow.

Standing in the coral sand,
the transition is striking,
as jade and emerald jewels in the shallows
yield to the turquoise and sapphires
of deeper waters where rainbow fish abound.

A ways out, piercing snow-white crests break
in a long arc that mirrors the shoreline,
signaling the edge of the reef,
beyond which the coral wall drops thousands of feet
into a black abyss.

I landed here on a wing and a whim
from a lingering northern winter,
and as the gentle trades blow,
and the sun warms my face,
I embrace the change in palette.

The iridescent cobalt glow,
is born of the water's absorption
of reds
and yellows
and oranges,
from the white light of the sun.
The blues then rise up from the coral sand
and light up the surface world
like a boundless source of energy.

So much color to give,
the pedestals of high billowing cumulus clouds to the south
turn blue and green themselves,
while to the north,
I blink,
and suspend disbelief that the hazy foundation of the sky
has taken on a pinkish hue,
even in bright, mid-day sun.

So much color to give,
the white bellies and under-wings
of the gulls dancing in flight
have taken on the cool aura of the ocean.

I again adjust my eyes as the sun takes a dip in the sea,
and smoldering embers anoint the western sky.
And as the light fades, and thunder rumbles across Grace Bay,
pink lightning arcs across a black lavender sky.

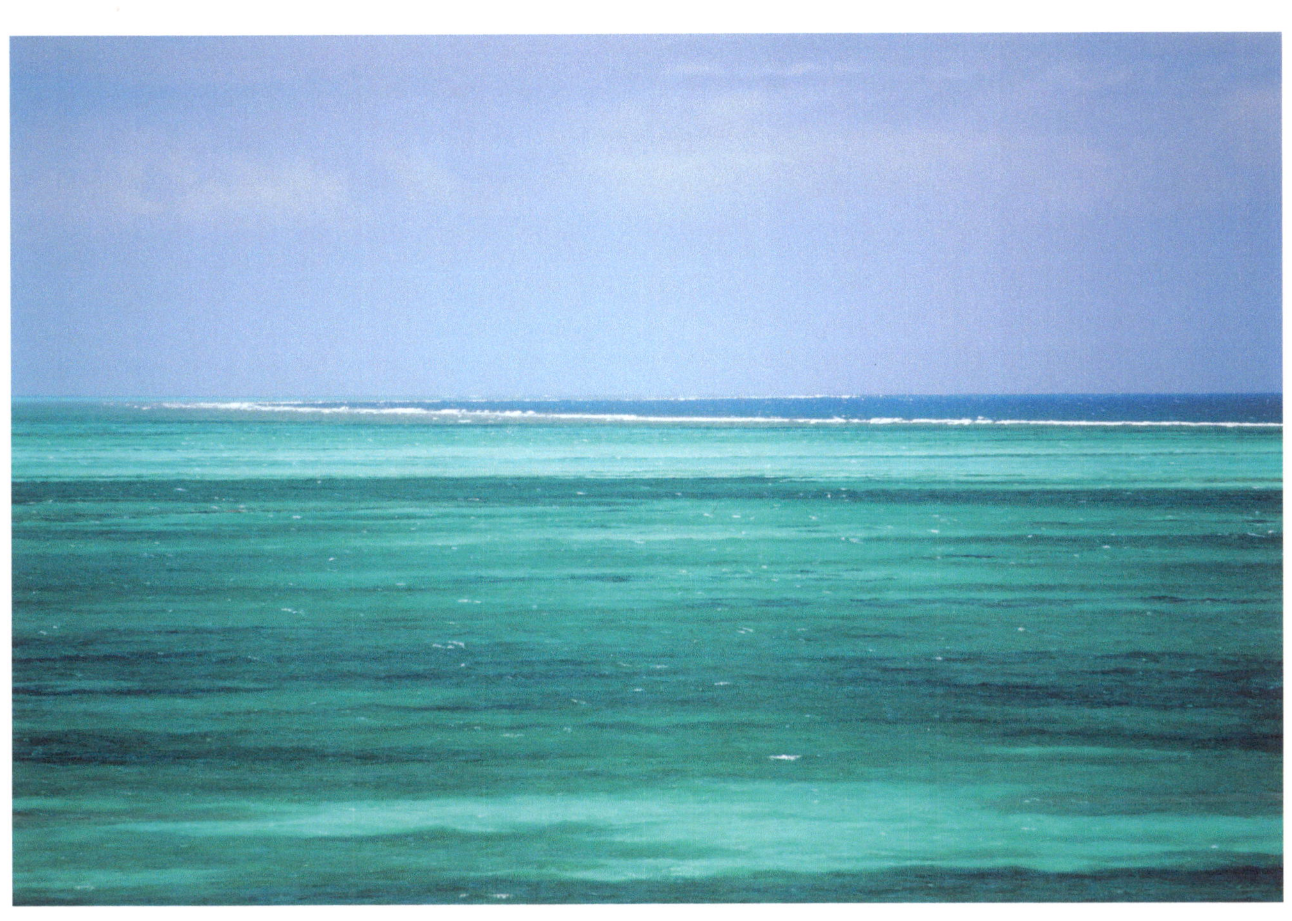

Kihei Waves

As dawn breaks, the sea is like glass,
its surface smooth from inaction,
no wind to speak of save for the soft brush
of a gentle trade wind breeze against my face.

Waves still advance upon the shore,
but their attempts to break impressively
are half-hearted at best,
just the occasional slap of a tiny curl.

Some waves wash up without a sound,
pushed by the invisible energy of sun and moon,
or an unseen squall
born thousands of miles away in Fiji or Polynesia.

First light in Kihei is pale,
as it takes some time
for the sun to rise
behind the massive sleeping giant, Haleakala.

As light finally touches the palms,
their outlines cast shadows
in the flat calm water.
This liquid glass is temporarily broken
by sleek outrigger canoes,
the stroke calling the pace,
his voice carrying across the water
to the beach.

Mid-day brings the wind,
and the waves respond,
growing up into large curls
that break with an incessant roar,
each line moving constantly up the shore,
changing in pitch from low to high
as the Doppler effect kicks in.

The high sun beats into the water,
lighting up the emerald greens and cobalt blues,
illuminating a sense of depth
beyond the break.

As the waves crest,
the peak is transparent enough to see through,
and for the briefest moment before breaking,
a blinding white line tops the crest.

On the back side, in the trough,
golden brown sand
billows up in columns,
as if rising smoke.

Then the wave crashes,
entraining the sugary sand
that liquefies beneath my feet.
For a moment, the glistening sands
reflect sea and sky,
before the water drains away,
retreating down to meet
the next incoming wave.

Swaying palm fronds,
inaudible at daybreak,
now tick, tick, tick, incessantly
as if with nervous energy.

As the sun fades into the sea
south of McGregor Point,
the ocean dances with bright golden light,
a path of diamonds
leading to the distant horizon.

The sun sets quickly in Kihei,
its finality marked by
the sounding of conch shells
carried on the breeze.

As the warm light fades to blue,
the waves return
to that familiar soothing rhythm
that lulls us to sleep,
just as it has done since the ancestors
sailed here from Polynesia,
just as it has done since the islands formed of fire
and rose up from the ocean floor.

The sound is all that remains,
the only clue to the waves existence,
as the night turns the sea
into a pitch-black canvas,
epic in the unseen,
broken only by the stars
that separate sea from sky.

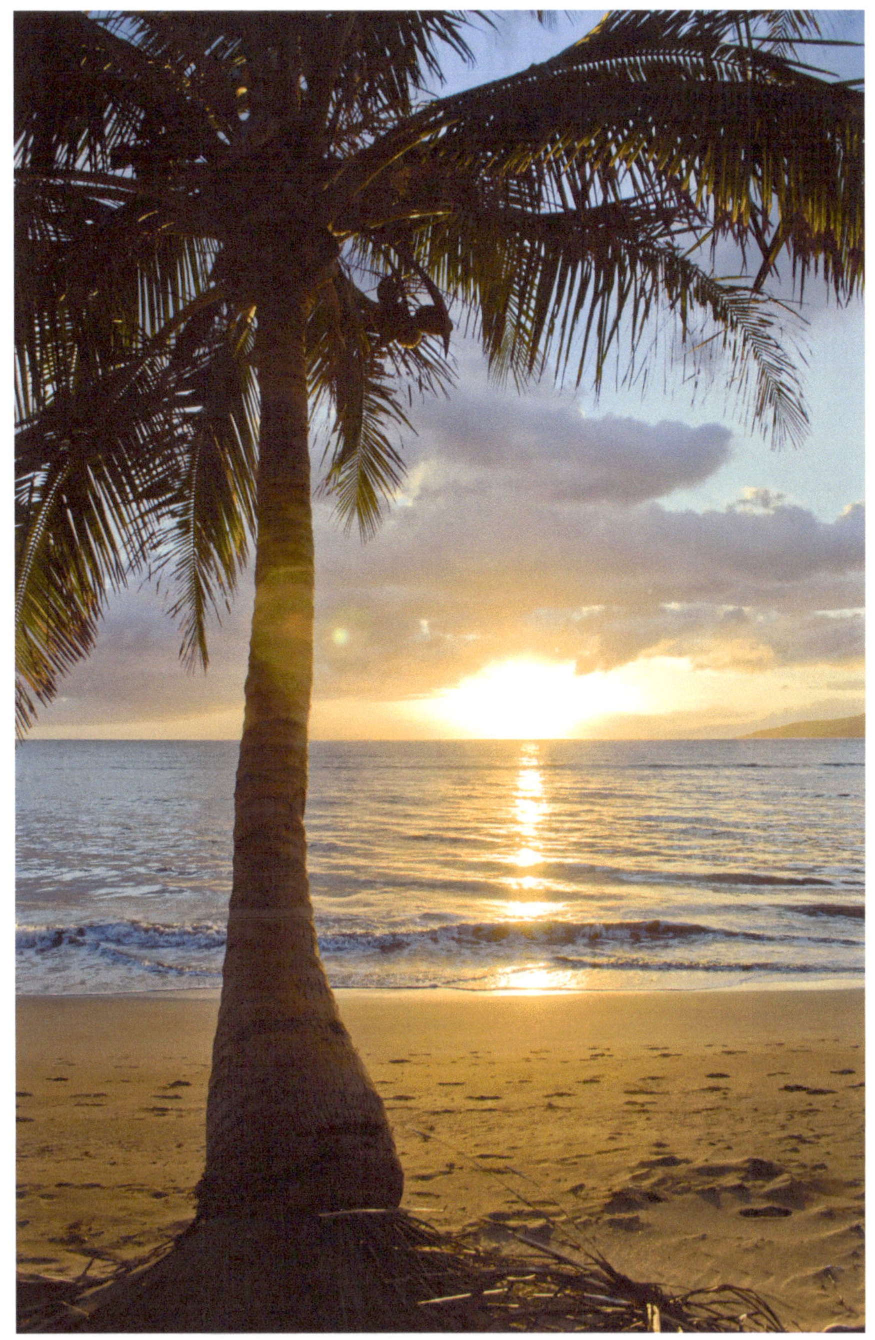

The Beauty in a Pebble

The pebble sits on the edge of the stream,
smooth and round,
rusty tan,
speckled with granitic gray and flecks of feldspar,
glinting brilliantly when the sun hits at just a certain angle.

Lying halfway submerged, neither wholly wet nor wholly dry,
the pebble sits silently,
cold clear water deflecting around each face,
rejoining below.

It is cradled in a gentle eddy,
as nearby the stream tumbles and froths,
churns and boils,
over craggy boulders and jammed logs.

The hydrologist
might tell of how the pebble traveled
from the Continental Divide
over thousands of years,
in spurts and starts,
with floods from spring snowmelt
and convective summer storms.
And how it may cascade
further downstream in future floods,
year after year,
and maybe one day,
(after I've returned to this earth as ash and dust),
find its way down the river to the sea,
if it doesn't turn to ash and dust.

The geologist
might tell of how the pebble is igneous in origin,
born of fire from the belly of the earth,
uplifted during the orogeny of the Rocky Mountains,
raised miles high into the air,
only to suffer the cracking and splitting and fracturing
during the endless freeze and thaw, freeze and thaw,
that breaks down a mountain into smaller and smaller bits.
And how it broke free of the mountain,
and found its way into a trickle of liquid life,
beginning its waltz with water down to the valleys below,
becoming more smooth and round with each passing mile.

The chemist
might tell of the slow dissolution
of the minerals
within its molecular matrix,
water being a universal solvent that can dissolve even rock.
And if there was calcite in the pebble,
how it would dissolve and consume carbon dioxide,
playing a role, however miniscule,
in regulating the temperature of the earth.

The physicist
might tell of how the pebble disturbs
the laminar flow in the stream,
and with its hard-cast neighbors,
creates turbulent flow
that slows the speed of the water,
lengthening its journey to the sea.
And how the turbulent energy speeds evaporation,
lifting water molecules into the air,
higher and higher,
until they merge into raindrops and fall
on the eastern plains, where cattle graze and crops grow.

The biologist
might tell of how the smooth surface of the pebble is not really smooth,
but is a world all its own,
containing imperceptible ridges and contours and hills and valleys
that provide a microscopic substrate for bits of algae to take hold,
using nutrients and sunlight to create life,
the base of a food chain that will cascade
through invertebrates, fish, and humans.

The astronomer
might tell of the pebble's true origins,
tracing much further back
than its breaking free of the Rockies,
back to its true beginnings some fourteen billion years ago, after the big bang.
And how the earth's primordial soup coalesced five billion years ago
from the solar nebula, a cloud of dust and gas,
leftovers of the feast that created the sun,
forming a core and a mantle and a crust
that continues to be molded and fissured,
eroded and reborn to this day,
and will continue until the sun expands hungrily into a red giant, consuming us.

Yet the pebble sits quiet and still,
being the only thing that it can be,
both monumental and insignificant in this moment,
beautiful in its very existence.

I sit quiet and still
and watch the smooth round pebble,
and I try to be
the only thing that I can be.

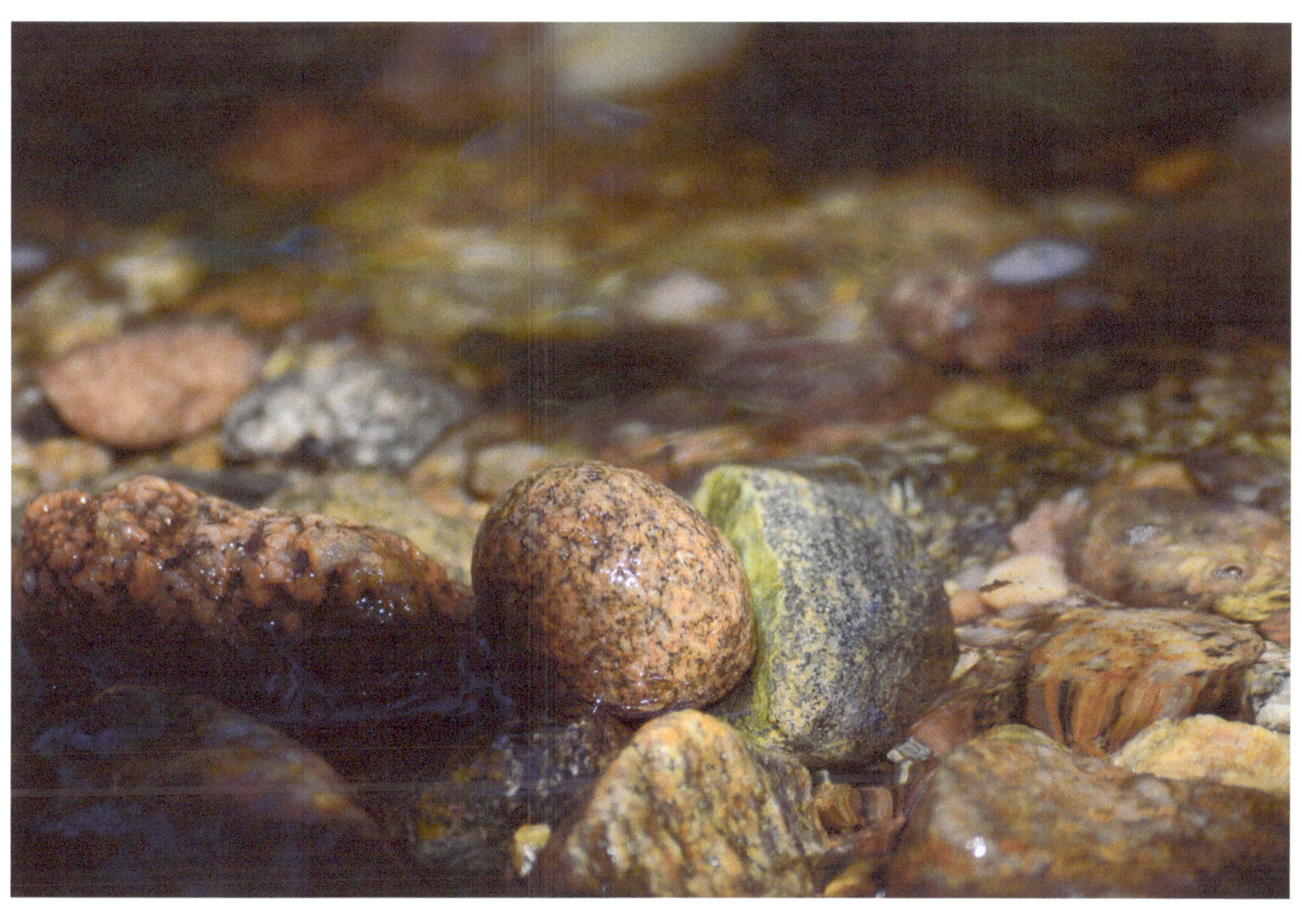

Whispers

And the cottonwood whispered to me,
and told me of his life in the peaceful pasture.

How he had sprouted as all trees do from the rich earth below,
and spread branches and leaves like open arms up into the endless sky.

The deer had come to browse on his shoots,
but he grew a thick shell of bark to protect his skin.

And he survived the arid, parched land,
sending roots deep into the ground,

where they drank
their lifeblood from Coal Creek.

And sometimes the Colorado sun baked hot,
but his leaves spread, and he grew tall and wide.

And the herd came now and then,
grazing in his presence, keeping him company.

And he weathered many a summer storm under billowing thunderheads,
with sizzling lightning cracks, and icy hail shredding his leaves.

And he weathered many a blizzard,
bending without breaking in the icy winter winds.

And life was good for a long, long time,
as it should be for a tree.

And he watched hawks soar on thermals
in the blue, blue sky.

And he listened to the song of redwing blackbirds,
sitting on cattails in the marsh just over there.

And at night he heard the coyotes howl
under roving constellations.

But as time passed, his bones grew brittle,
and his leaves could no longer pull in the sun.

And the wind and the snow
broke his old branches.

Yet he still whispers to me,
and the herd still grazes in his shadow.

And the hawks still soar,
and the blackbirds still sing.

And the pasture is still at peace.

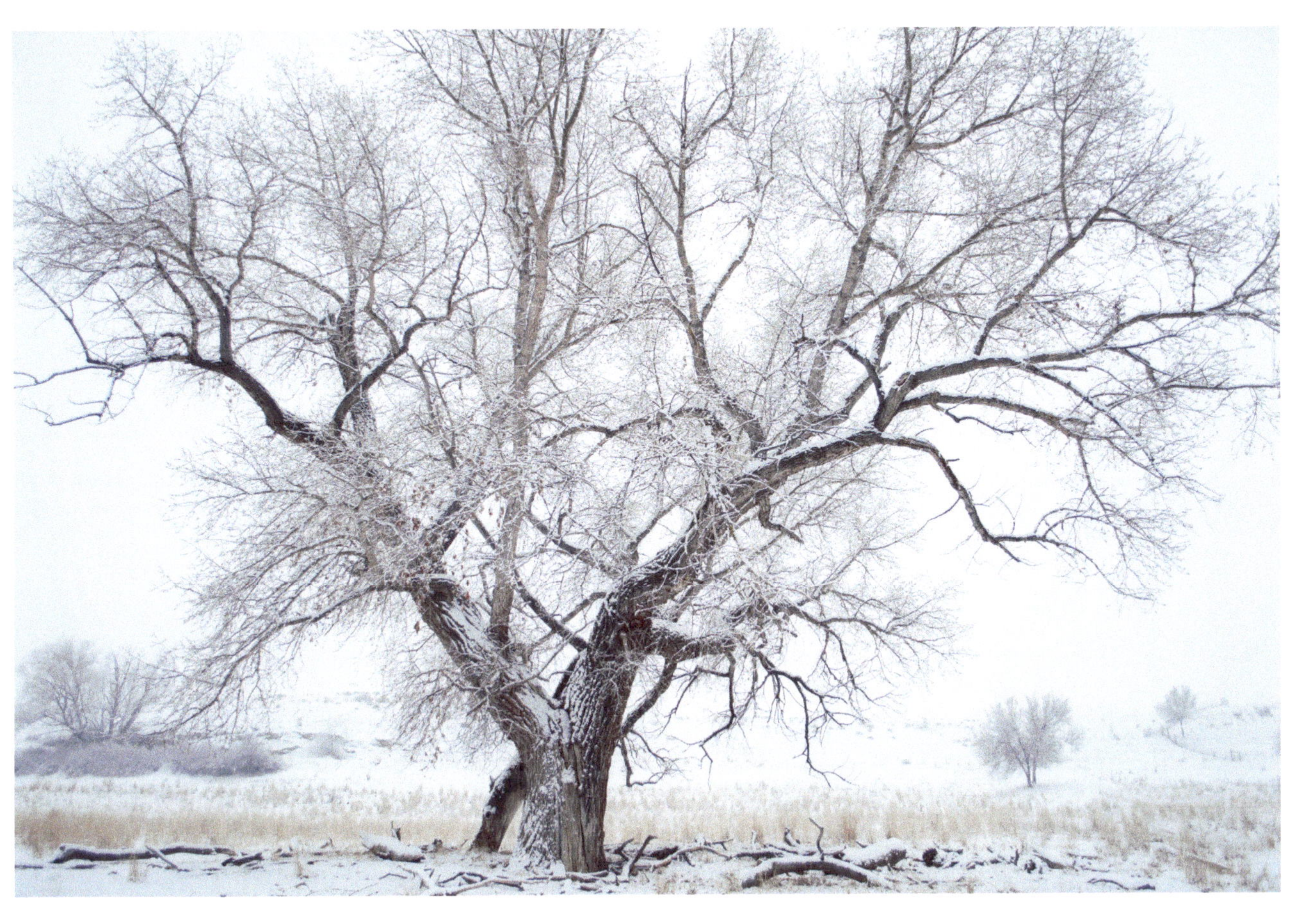

Chapter 5 - Moments

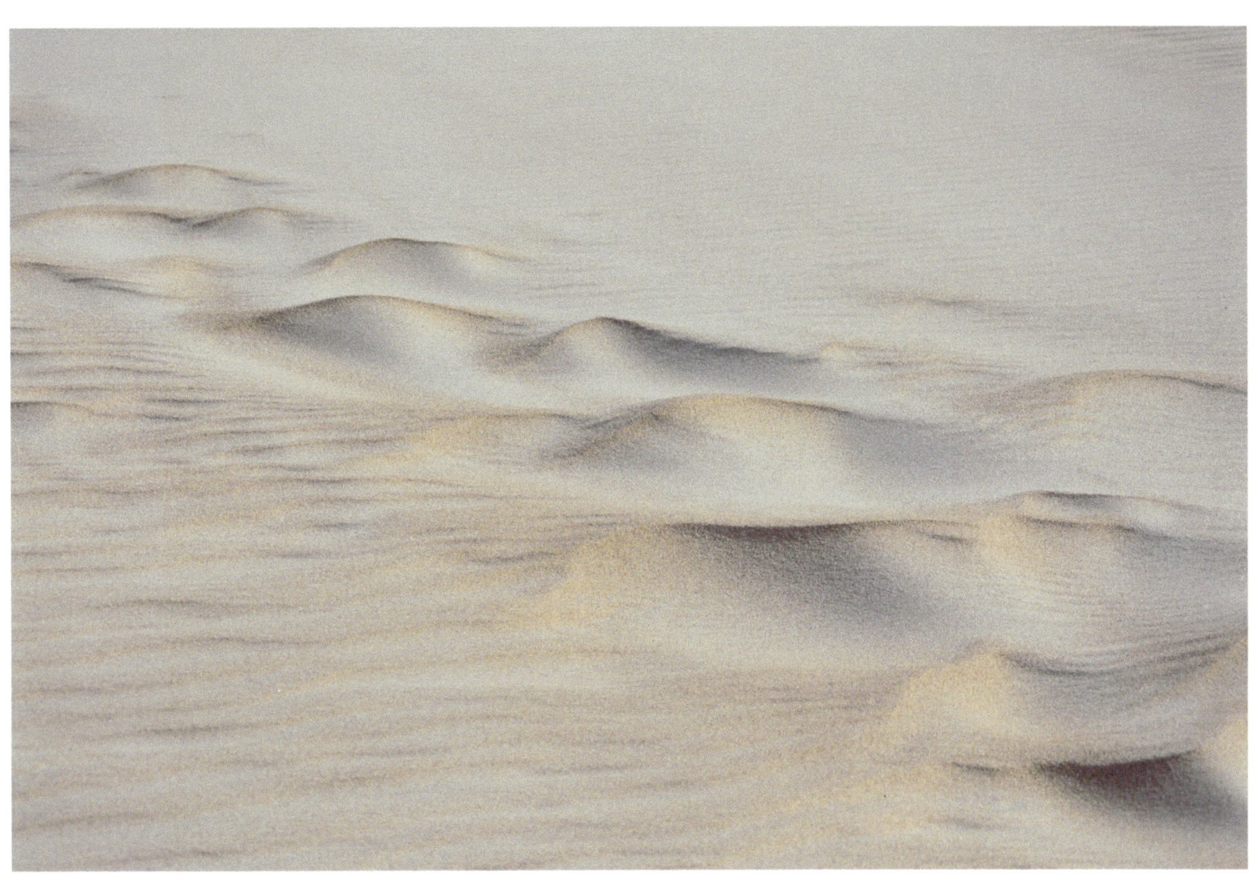

Driftless

I wander the Wisconsin Driftless Area,
a land unscathed
by the advance of glaciers,
but not the advance of time.

The Mississippi flows inevitably downhill,
carving the continent below buff-colored bluffs.
As I walk this path I leave only footprints,
an ephemeral trace of my existence.

Maple leaves drift to the ground.
No strength left to hang on to their limbs
under blustery winds from the north,
they tumble and scatter like scarlet snowflakes.

As new mountains rise from the ashes of old,
these fragile limestone bluffs
will gradually erode and be forgotten,
save for the geological record of the earth.

And as the last rays of golden light reflect across this river of glass,
I know from whence it came, and I know its final fate.
But I sit and watch the river drift below me,
for its time is now.

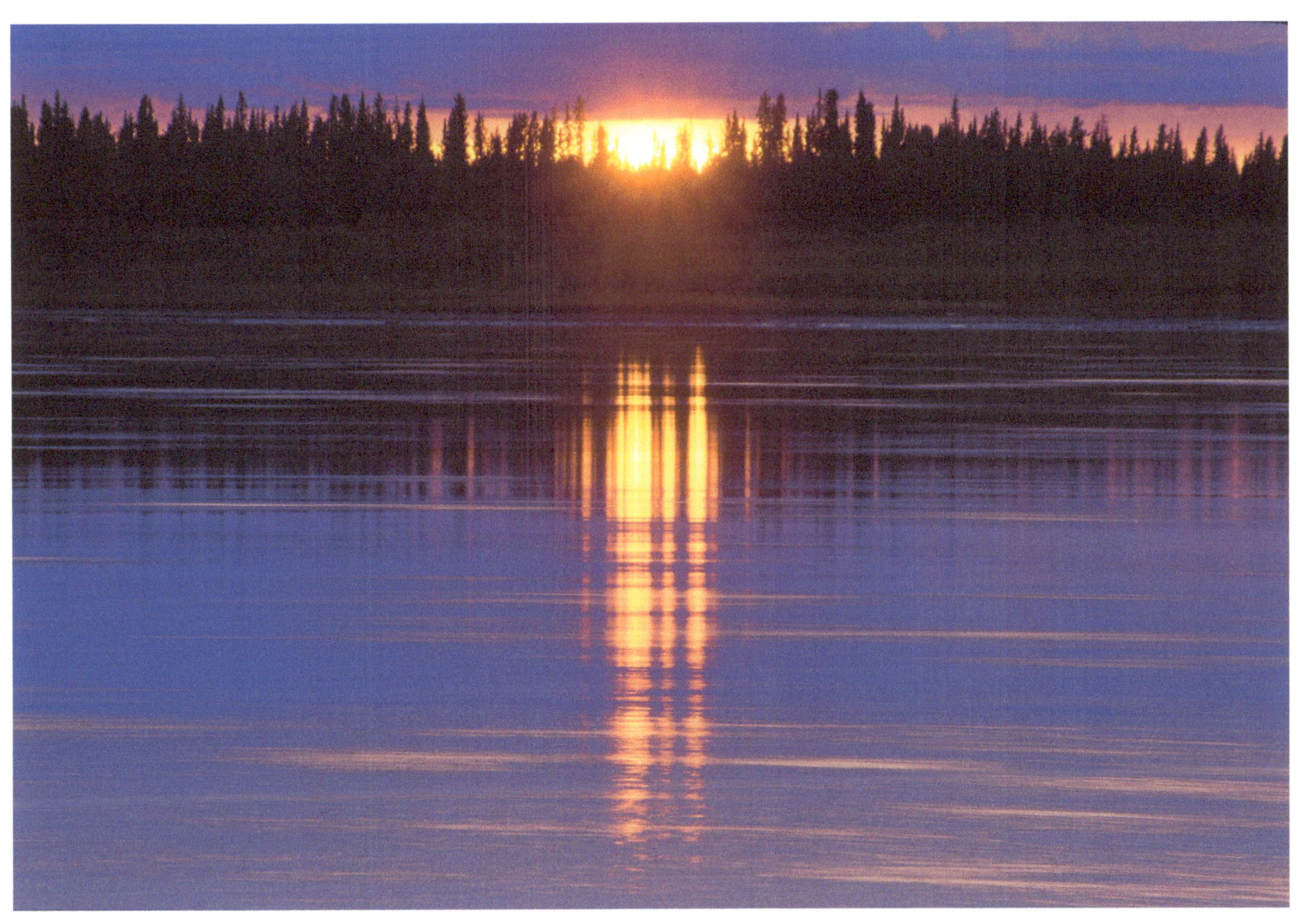

Wisconsin Highlands

I long for the stillness of a Wisconsin Highlands early evening.

No sound,
 but the occasional scamper of a chipmunk or squirrel
 across the crusty surface of late spring snowpack,
 or the distant staccato tapping of a woodpecker.

Night approaching,
 my breath is frosty, though I can feel
 Winter has lost her edge.

White tail deer tracks,
 once distinct in the deep snow,
 have begun to subside into random depressions from mid-day sun.

Down through the woods,
 the lake is still frozen,
 though a sinuous moat is beginning to grow along its shoreline perimeter.

The sky in fading light turns a deeper, darker blue before my eyes.

Leafless branches,
 appearing as inky black etchings, stand starkly against the sky,
 then slowly fade from view, as a tapestry of stars appear
 expressing the vastness of the universe.

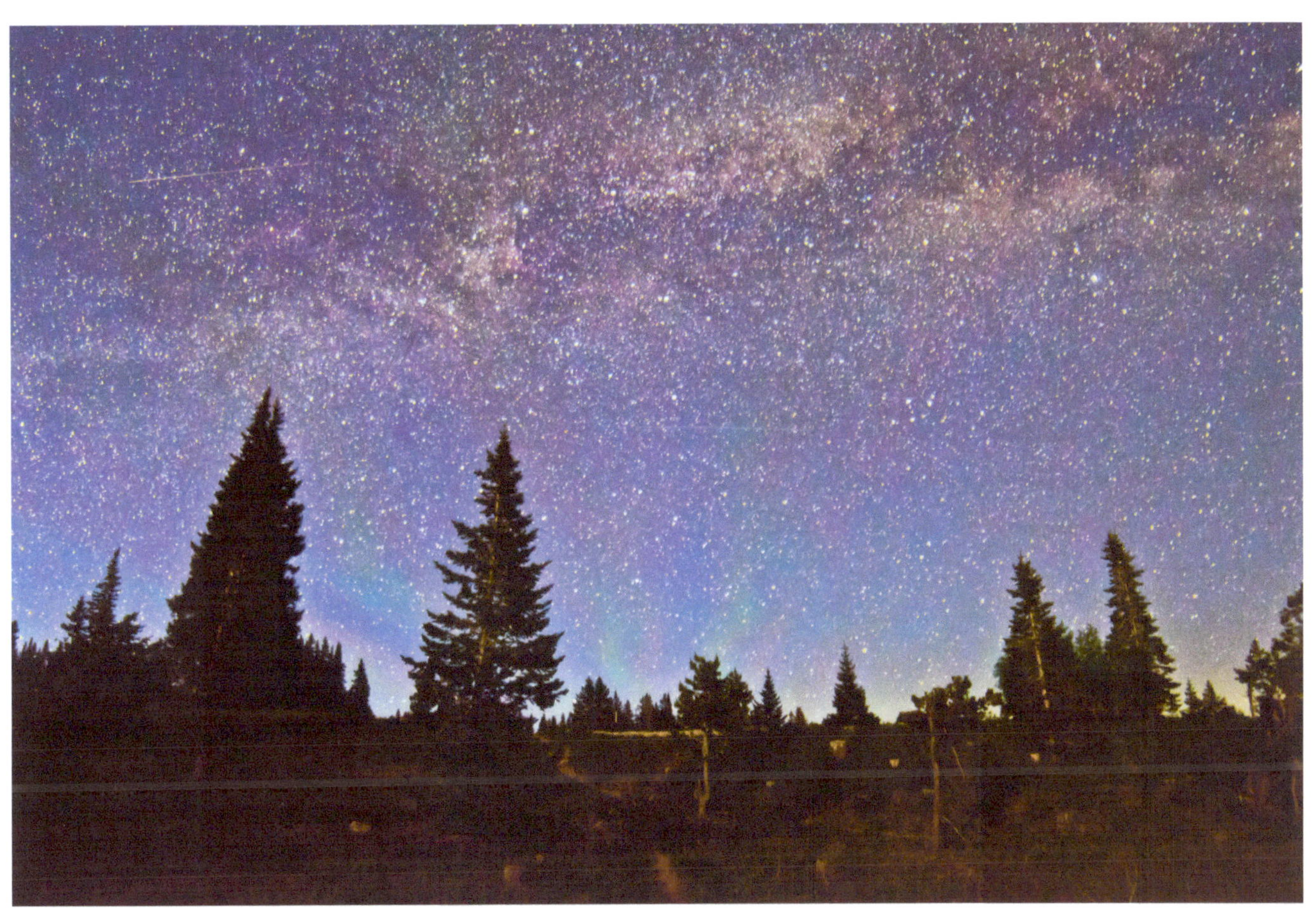

Whose Shade I'll Never See

When I rise slowly
and stumble in the dark

When my path is clear
though my steps unsteady

When the light fades
and ghosts whisper my name

I will plant a tree
whose shade I'll never see

And that is how it should be

But for now,

I will tend my garden
with a loving hand

I will water and prune,
and nurture the soil

I will protect fragile shoots
when storms threaten

I will listen when the flowers
have something to say

And that is how it should be

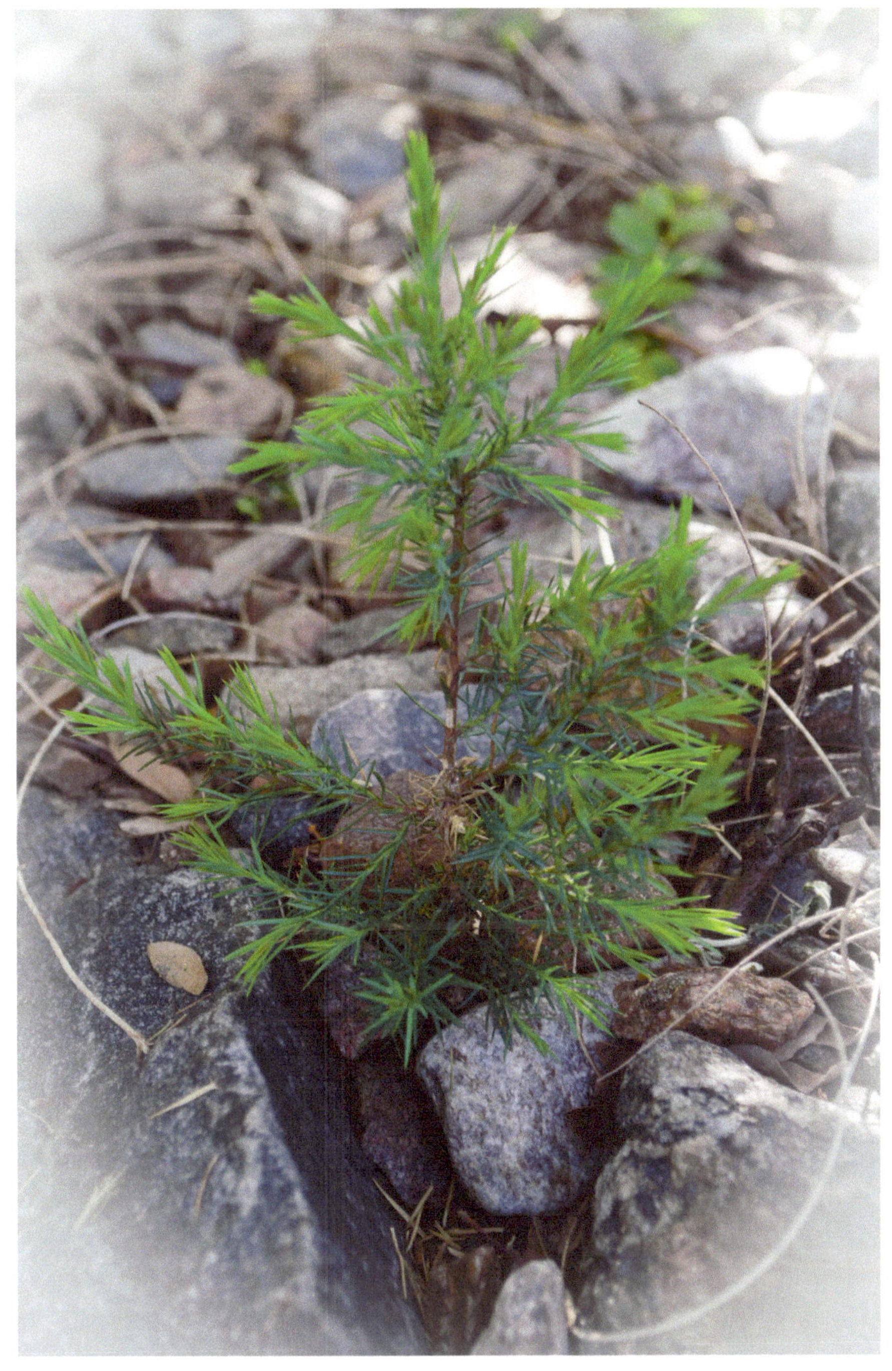

Some Leaves

Some leaves fall much too soon,
still green and in their prime.
No outward sign of disease, they still
succumb before their time.

Some leaves blow away in storms
or wither on the vine.
All manner of ills can befall
without reason or rhyme.

Some leaves settle down to earth
at just the perfect moment.
Glowing and bathed in warm soft light,
no signs of inner torment.

Some leaves simply hang on too long,
become withered, brittle, and brown.
Unwilling to fall until cold of winter
and fresh snow blankets the ground.

Autumn surely is coming now,
the days are not so long.
I lie awake in bed at night,
at the wonder of my song.

I wonder what leaf I will be
on this particular tree.
And holding her desired place,
what of the leaf beside me?

Weathering the seasons,
and weathering the storms,
We've bathed in sun and starlight
since the day that we were born.

I hope we fall together,
arm in arm on a gentle breeze,
come to rest in rich brown earth,
and nurture future trees.

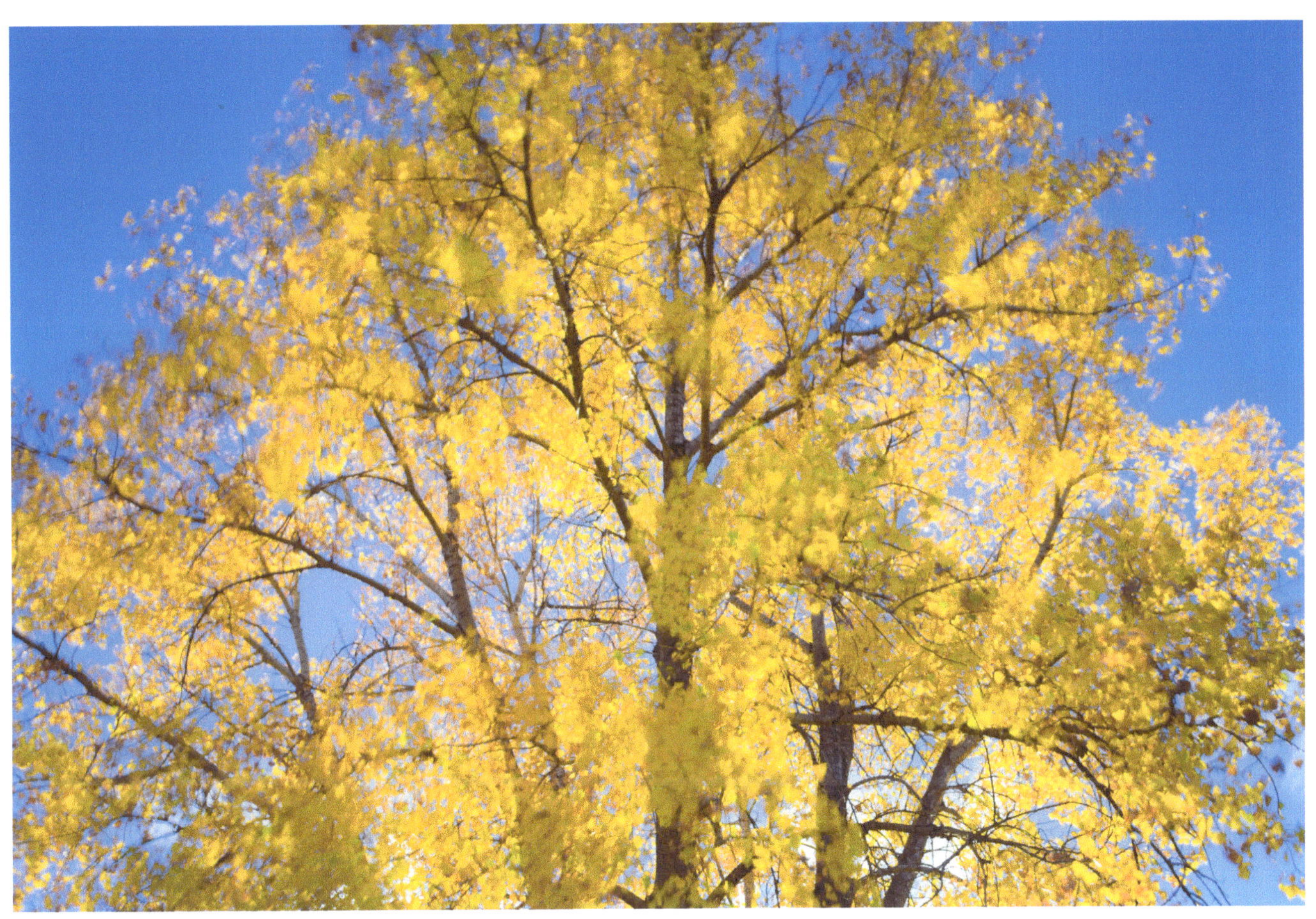

The Mariner's Mirage

There is a pleasant, gentle warmth
at the end of the day.
After the hot, white light
of the mid-day arc
has baked the skin,
and blinded the eyes,
and scorched the sand
beneath my feet,
turning a stroll
into something
all but unbearable.

The minute crystalline quartz
of the wide and graceful beach,
eroded over the eons,
sharp under the scope,
though smooth running through my fingers,
now welcomes my path.

The metronomic waves,
bowing to the wind,
and the currents,
and the tides,
and gravity,
now lap gently at my feet.

No longer star white,
the light now refracts
as through a crystal prism,
and with open arms,
embraces me,
with harmonious chords
of coral, vermillion, and amber.

And now I wait.

When the sky's knowing eye,
red hot from fusion's fire,
first connects with the sea,
it bleeds out along horizon's rule,
like molten steel
being poured into a cast.

The sun appears to sink faster
as Helios yields to Erebus,
faster than it seems
across the arc of a day,
now that the horizon provides
a tangible frame of reference.

I wait, hoping,
that as the last bit of glowing embers
extinguish beneath the sea,
I will see,
if I don't blink,
the fleeting green flash,
the mariner's mirage.

But I do not see.

Again, and again,
day after day,
I stand,
and wait,
and hope,
and try,
but I do not see
the mythical light.

And perhaps that is the point.
Again, and again,
day after day,
I stand,
and wait,
and hope,
and try.

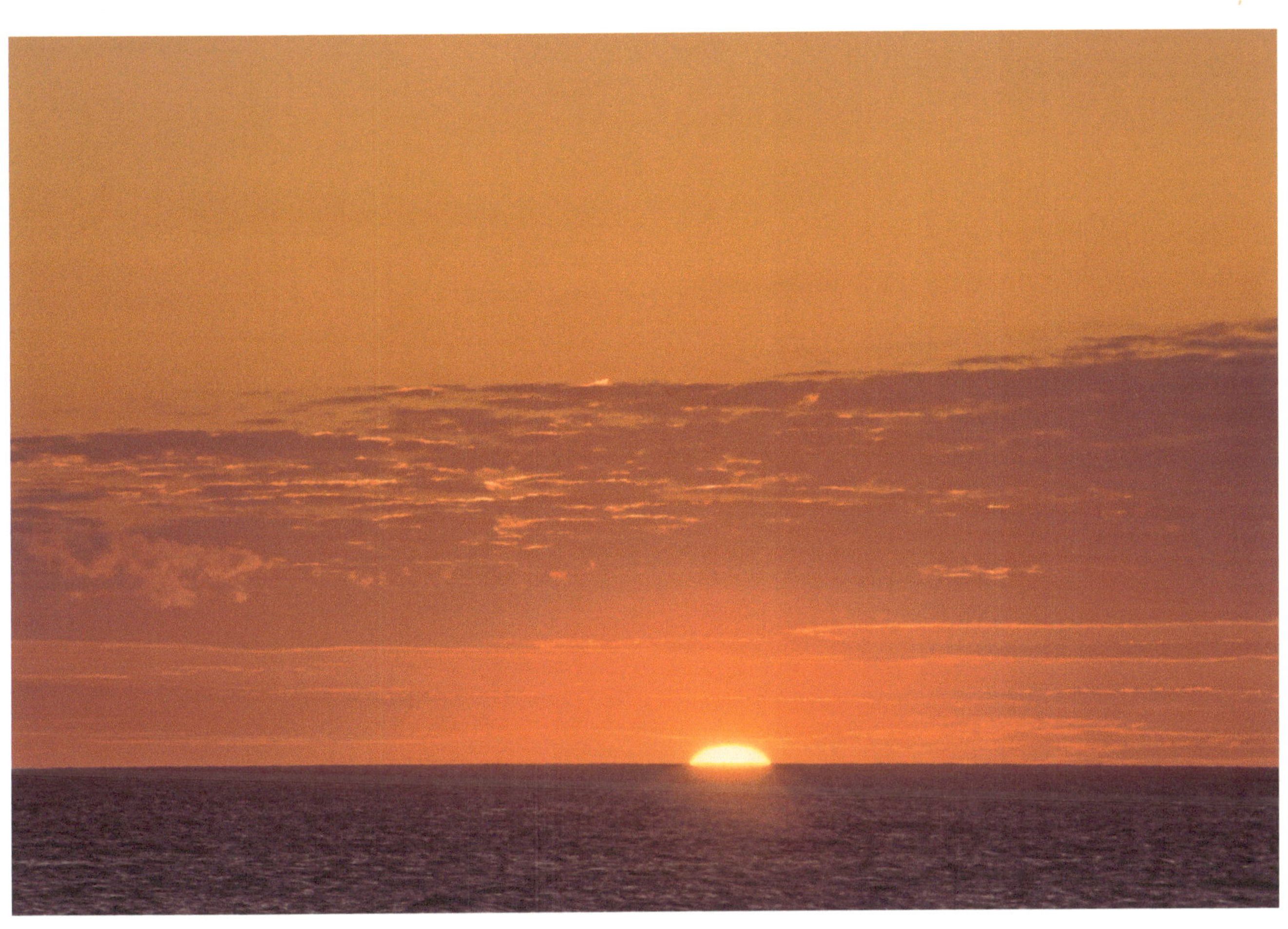

Cerrillos

Old Joe is kicking up dust,
and I ease back on the reins to let it settle.

I can hear the Sunday bells
from Iglesia de San Jose,
the invitation carried on the breeze,
up into the small hills
for which the town was named.

But I commune under the endless New Mexico sky,
surrounded by the spirits of
the Tano Indians who came before me.
I sit high in my worn leather pew,
and listen in reverence to what the
Sangre de Cristos have to tell me.

The summer heat presses down from the heavens
like gravity itself,
the sky filled with a hot blue flame.
Piñon and juniper and sage
fill the dry desert air like incense.

Joe snorts and scuffs his shoe,
itching to get back.
I ease him along,
triggering a skittish rattler,
but Joe pays it no mind.

His shoes clomp up the hard sandstone
on the backside of the dusty arroyo,
a few revenant red cholla blooms
guiding our way.

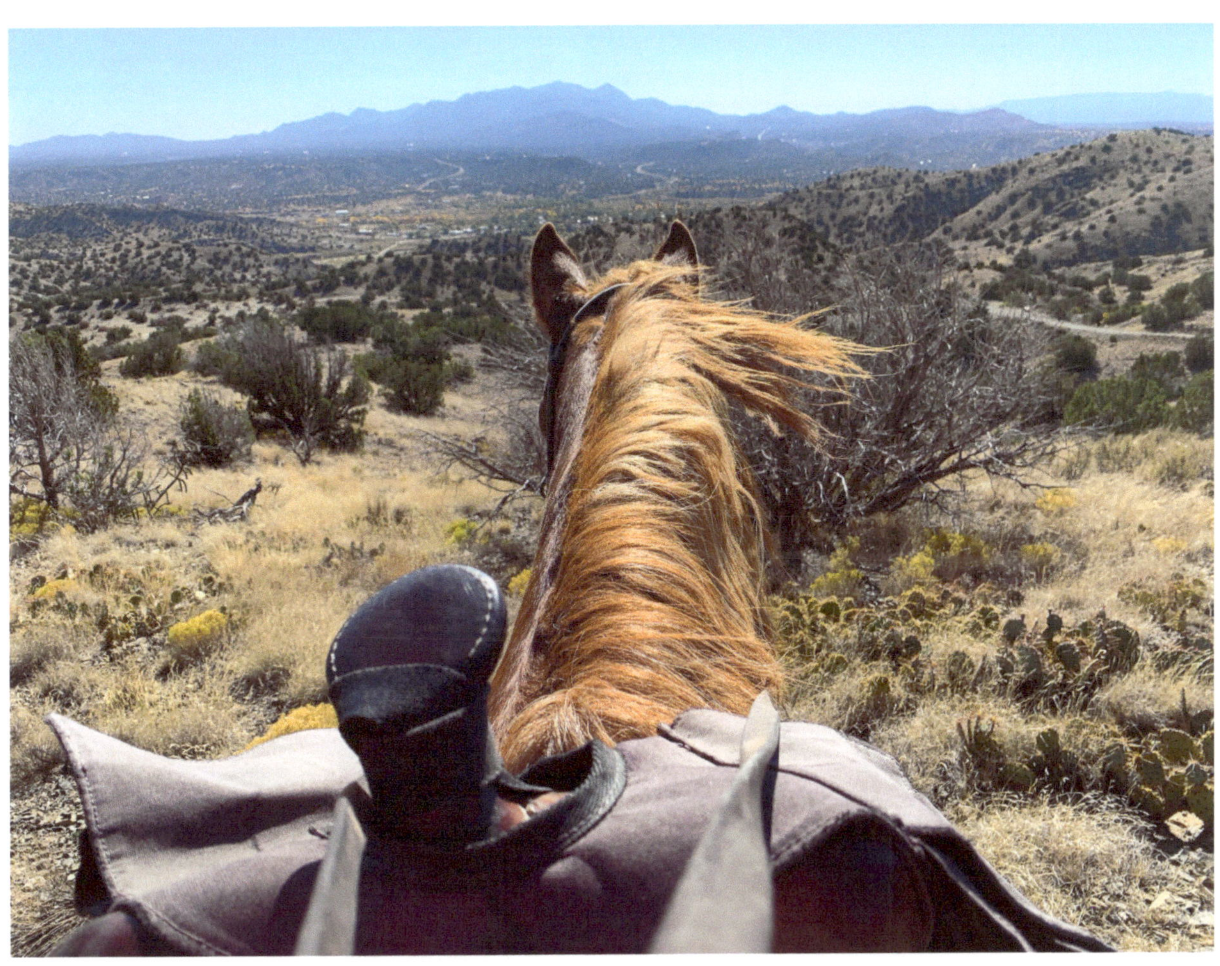

Chapter 6 - Home

Seeds

In the high plains and parks of Colorado,
seeds, as if snow, release from their cottonwood canopy,
drifting down through lush leaves that
bow, sway, and quake under gentle summer breezes.

Back-lit by a white sun,
the glowing seeds come in waves,
crossing the ocean of blue above me,
seeking to grab hold,
to hang on,
to gain purchase,
on some new plot of land.

Most will not survive,
the air too hot, the soil too dry,
the spot already taken
by another established tree.

Some drift into raging creeks,
waters bank-full of snowmelt from the high country,
their destination the Gulf or Pacific,
their fate decided by the continental divide.

Riding currents of air or water with little control,
they hope to come to rest
in some beautiful patch of organic detritus,
where they can establish roots and grow.

Ancient DNA compels us all
to find our place in this world,
a place to call home,
a place to continue to be.

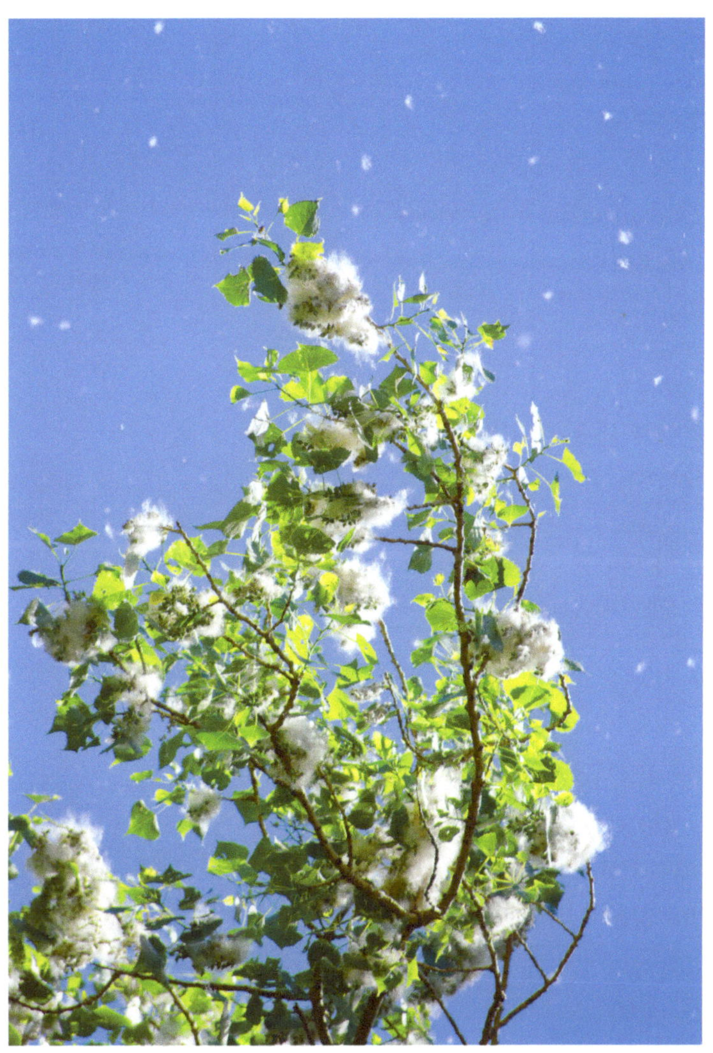

Outer Banks

Standing in the surf,
in the pale gray light of dawn,
the tide is coming in,
the most primordial of timekeepers.

Water rushes past me.

As they return to the sea,
wave after wave
begins to eat away
at the loose liquid sand below.

Balance is required,
as grain by grain,
my foundation is eroded away.
I begin to sink under my own pressing weight.

Stay too long in one place,
and be buried, or drowned,
or carried out to sea
against your will.

It should be just physics, really.
The gravity of the moon and sun,
the turbulence of wind and waves,
and the geomorphology of the earth.

But in the maelstrom of life,
Chaos theory reigns.
Each wave crashing, every ripple swirling,
interacts in ways that confound prediction,
propagating out in space and time,
toward an uncertain future.

To know the future would be to stand in place, unmoving,
ankle-deep in the thick soup of ancient earth.
To move, to adapt, is to survive,
to live to see another beautiful daybreak.

Tomorrow provides another chance
to chart a course
across the great pewter green sea,
somewhere beyond the visible horizon.

And yet, someone drowned here yesterday.
A savior briefly held his hand,
but opposing forces separated them,
and the man was never seen again.

You can drown if you stay too long in one place,
and you can drown if you venture too far.

A hurricane is approaching.
Stay put, ride it out, take your chances,
or heed the red flag warnings,
pull your feet out of the sand,
and head for higher ground.

My internal compass spins erratically.
North or south?
Stay or leave?
Sink or swim?

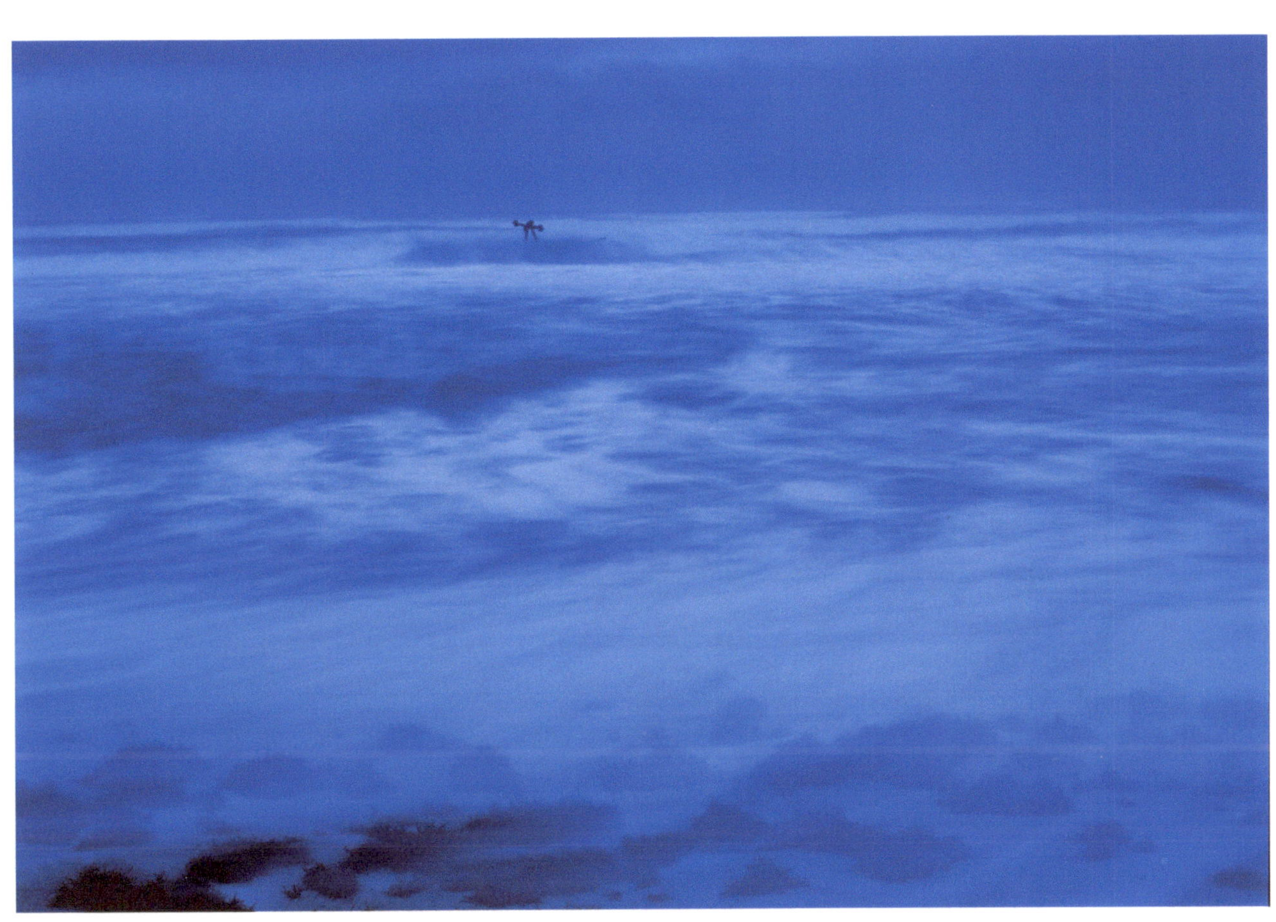

Canvasback Lake

The mornings, now, carry a chill
down from the high Arctic,
and fog hangs like a cottony blanket
over the still-warm lake.

A golden sun slowly disperses the simmering mist,
and the afternoons warm,
and I can still feel the heat
on my skin.

Change happens quickly up here,
and I now lose an hour of light a week,
a trend that will continue unabated
until perpetual night sinks in from the heavens.

I've already pushed
the envelope of my stay,
risked being stranded if my ride out
can't make it through the White Mountains.

I can't stay – I know that.
I wish I were there –
I wish you were here.

I take the boat out for one last ride in the low late light,
slicing through the glassy surface.
The sun travels in a crazy low arc around the sky,
as if tethered to the horizon.

My foray across the lake
seems almost an invasion, or intrusion,
and I try to be as quiet as I can,
out of respect.

In the faintest thought of a breeze,
scores of tiny spiders drift
on whispering strands of silk,
coming to rest in a new patch of bulrush
along the shore.

The canvasbacks and shovelers
remain on the lake,
the arctic terns of summer having already left,
heading out on their long long journey south,
on a seemingly endless migration,
no place to call home.

Below the hull
lies a universe all its own.
Multitudes of tiny shrimp
and other nameless creatures
swim in a seemingly random fashion,
sailing through intricate columns
of algae and mosses,
the "pillars of creation" in
the vast sky below me.

Down on the dock,
after dinner,
I watch the black, slick-haired muskrats
swim silently around the cove,
then make a quick splash
and a dive when they eye me
on my perch above the water.

The ducks squabble, and feed,
and I can hear their wings flapping
from quite a ways away through the still air,
while somewhere in the distance,
loons call out into the growing darkness
with a mournful wail.

A full, blood orange moon rises over the lake,
setting a perfect reflection on the water,
broken only by a duck or muskrat
that crosses its beam.

Last night the moon rose fifteen degrees to the south,
and I've noticed that the trajectories of the sun and moon
have thrown off my internal compass,
requiring an almost daily recalibration
of my sense of place.

Under chilly stars,
I wake and return to the dock,
to watch aurora's dance.

"Starry Night" swirls of white smoke arc across the sky.
Billowing curtains from the invisible solar wind
shimmer under the Big Bear,
while virga rain of electrons and protons fall
and tendrils of red and green shoot down to the west,
raining fire over my cabin.

Now I sit in the sun on the dock
one last time,
just watching and listening,
the aspen behind me on shore
quaking as if it knows what's coming,
leaves the color of the sun
drifting down around me
like falling stars.

I take a sip of whiskey,
my traditional toast to the lake.

I've brought the boat up, and secured it.
I've lowered the heavy shutters on their pulleys,
and closed the latches,
and pulled the thick wooden door closed -
both shutters and door have nails protruding out
to deter curious sniffing bears.

I hear the Cessna 185 approaching long before I see it,
a low hum that cuts through the breathless sky.
It's a breach of the all-enveloping silence it left me alone with,
several full moons ago.

Then there is the roar
as the floats set down on my quiet lake,
skipping like a stone before the plane settles in,
and taxis over to the dock.

Minutes later, the pilot accelerates,
and tips his wing,
to break the surface tension that holds the floats
like the grip that the lake holds over me,
and we break free,
turning the compass south,
towards home.

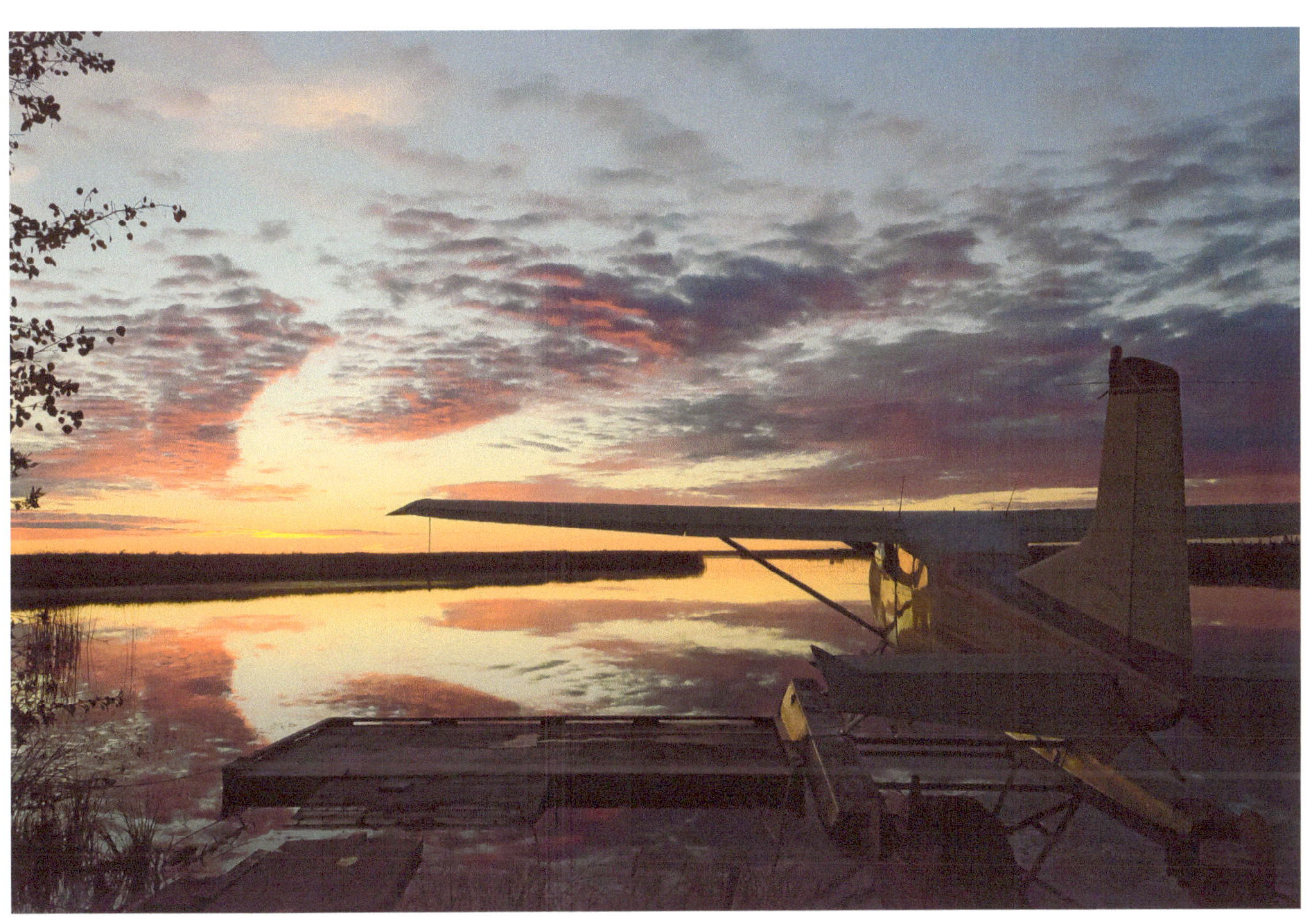

Echoes

The stair boards creak under my father's weight in the dark of early morning.
The hum of the furnace rises from the basement.
The iron radiators clank and ping as he bleeds air from the ageing pipes,
    bringing heat once again to my bedroom over the garage.
My bed sags, and the springs squeak,
    and muffled voices drift in from behind the cracked door down the hall.
Sounds of safety and security echo through this old house.

A thousand miles away,
    the stair boards creak under my weight in the dark of early morning...

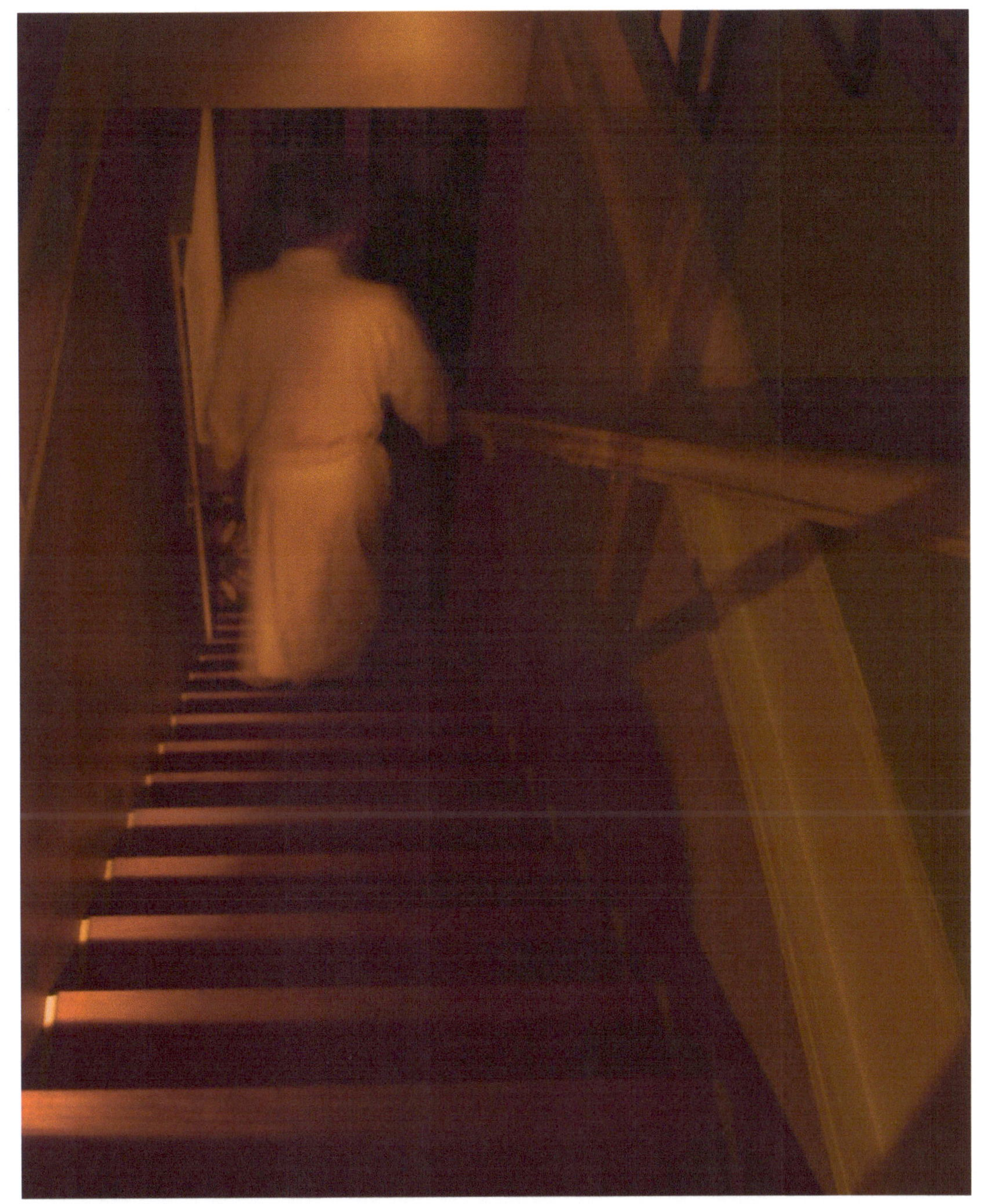

Searching For Light

The gnarled, old bigleaf maples
in the Hoh rainforest of Washington
spread moss-covered branches out every which way,
some even bending and bowing downward towards the rich soil,
trying to divine the source of life-giving sun.

Ancient sequoias tower hundreds of feet,
stretching their stalwart forms,
their crowns reaching
deep into the California sky.

In Fishlake Forest in Utah,
the Pando Grove of aspen,
the "trembling giant,"
is the largest organism on earth,
a single clone covering a hundred acres of land.

Though silent to our ears,
trees communicate with their neighbors,
even with those of different species,
exchanging nutrients, defense signals,
and wisdom.

Through their deep entwined roots,
they establish a rich, interdependent community,
full of symbiotic relationships
that promote adaption and resilience
throughout the entire forest.

I stand, silent and solemn
amongst the trees,
and realize,
we are all just searching for light.

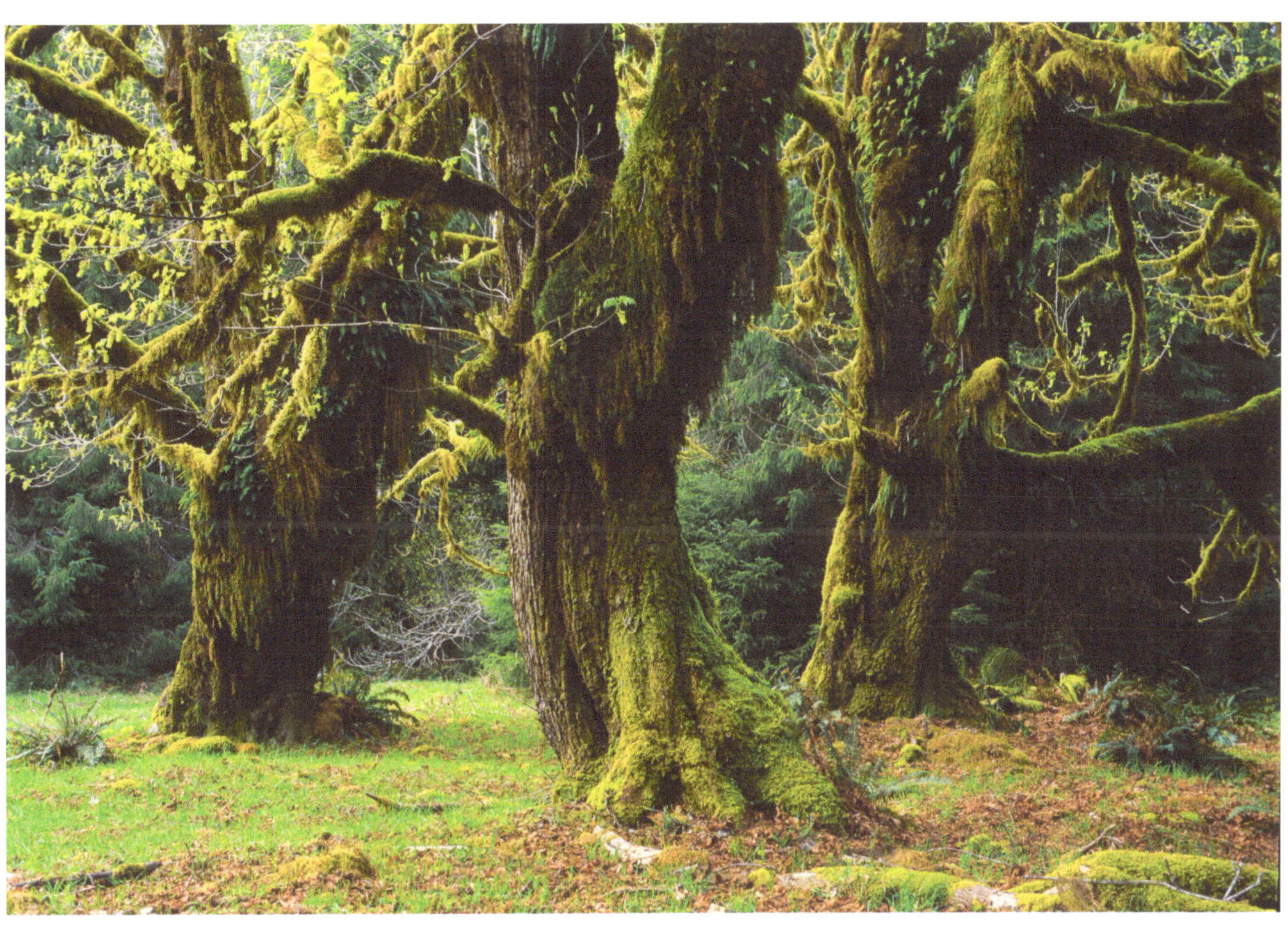

So Close to Home

The farmer is so close to home.
The mournful wail of the freight locomotive enters with the night
through the open window in the cab of his truck.
The flashing light at the crossing warns him off the tracks.
The harvest had run day and night,
an endless repetition,
up one set of rows and then down the next,
never ending until the bins were full of ripe grain.
He stares at the flashing light, exhausted,
and wonders whether he will get a fair price.
Finally, he slips past the tracks
and eases his truck up against the barn.

The fisherman is so close to home.
The lonesome wail of the foghorn enters with the night
through the open window of his wheelhouse.
The flashing light of the lighthouse on the point warns him off the shoals.
The harvest had run day and night,
an endless repetition,
up one line set and down the next,
never ending until the holds were full of fish on ice.
He stares at the flashing light, exhausted,
and wonders whether he will get a fair price.
Finally, he slips past the breakwater
and eases his boat up against the dock.

They call to me in the middle of the night,
so strange now after all of the miles I've traveled.
I get up, and I wander through the dark
to harvest my thoughts,
hoping to lay the weary travelers to rest.
I navigate by memory in the pitch black,
though slivers of moonlight thread through
the winter trees, guiding me as I
slip quietly back into bed.

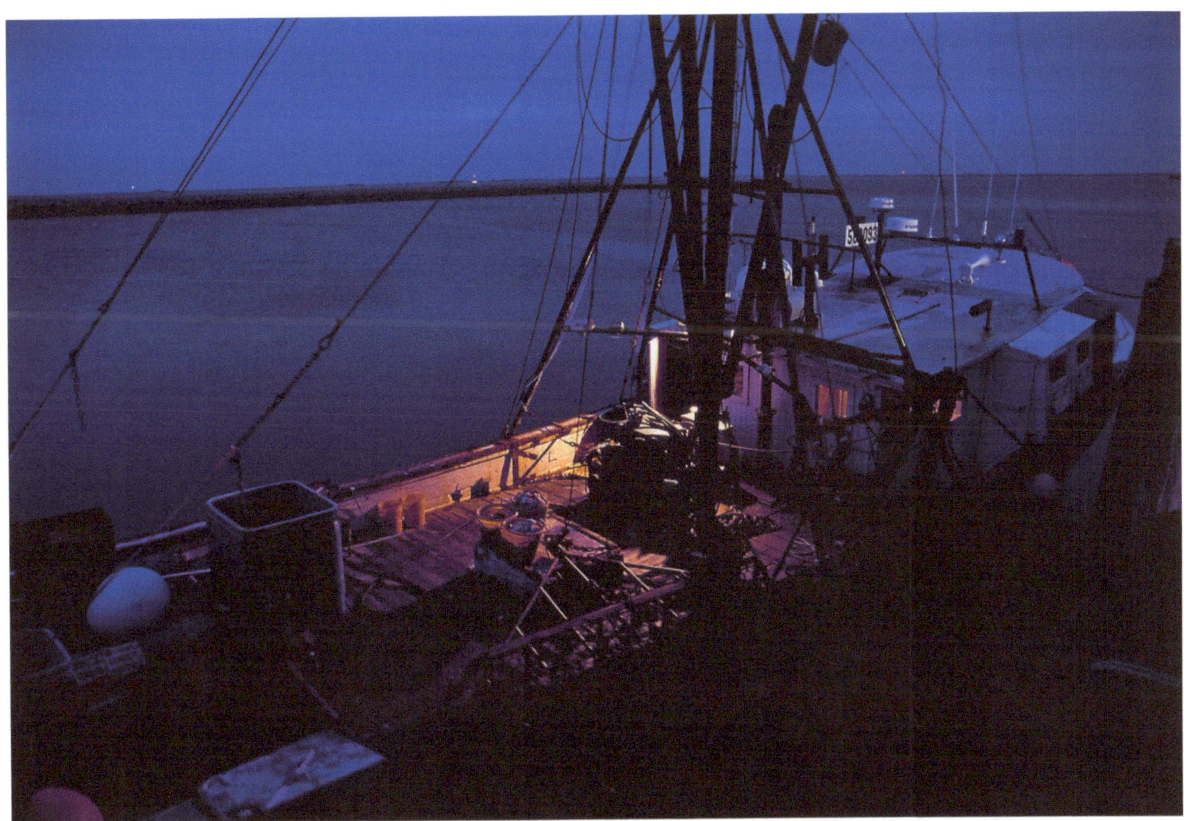

Dawn's Gate

My eyes open to darkness.
The house is still and asleep,
though the distant sound of easy, gentle breakers
drifts up through the ether to the open window.

The pre-dawn air, cool and dewy,
leads the wisps of white lace curtain
like a silent partner
in a graceful minuet.

The musty pine creaks
like an old ghost
as I make my way, toe-heel,
down the dark hallway.

Fog envelops the house
like a shroud,
the goddess Achlys
unwilling to surrender
night to day.

The gray boardwalk,
cracked and uneven,
leads across the whispering dune grass
to the weathered gate.

Beyond lies a steep precipice,
and a hidden staircase
that descends to
the deserted beach.

The precipice has advanced
closer and closer to the gate,
as each waltz around the sun
has brought furious winter gales
that have torn away at the fragile dune cliff,
each layer of sand sloughing off
as if dead skin,
to be picked up by Poseidon
and buried at sea.

Each passing,
each avalanche of sand,
brings us closer
to the brink.

And the house,
whose foundation
once solid and sure,
will one day yield
to the undertow,
and will tumble ungainly
to the beach below,
breaking joints,
tearing muscle,
losing power,
and water,
and wooden heartbeat,
joining the flotsam and jetsam
that the feckless moon and tide
had washed up hours before.

Yet the gate still holds its ground,
as just at this moment
a smoky ball of fire and light
emerges from behind the curtain of fog.

I walk the planks to the gate,
close the rusty latch behind me,
and descend into the warmth
of a new day.

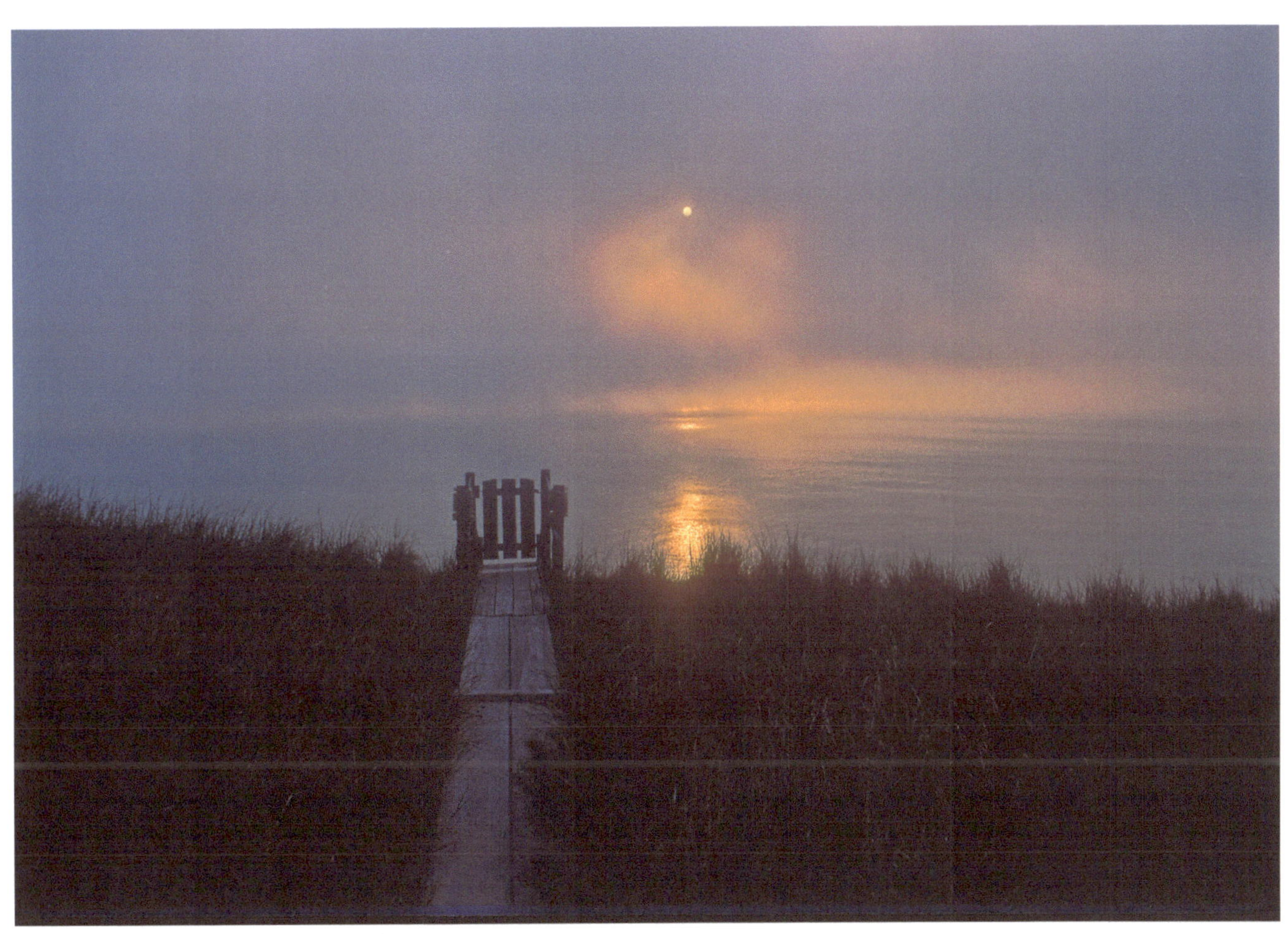

Acknowledgments

My enormous gratitude to...

Paul Fohrman, for his creative cover design, Photoshop work on the "Chairs of Stone" photo, and for collaboration on my poem, "The Edge." He is the Nurturer of Inner Peace and a thoughtful sounding board partner for all things poetry, photography, and music.

Tom Prescott, for his insightful editorial comments, text and photo formatting, and design for publication. A multi-talented artist, writer, and photographer, he is the college brother I never knew I had until we met all those years ago.

The McCleskey family, for help in setting up the "Echoes" photo and for their never-ending support. My biggest photography collectors and exceptional traveling companions, they are as close to family as you can get. Life would be a lot less fun without them.

Mike and Kate, good friends and SCUBA buddies, for help in setting up the photo for "The Edge" poem on a blustery Boulder day. We could barely keep the tripod on the ground as Mike peeled away in his pickup for the shot. It took several attempts, but I got the conceptual image I was looking for.

Fellow poet Cristina Olsen, for her invaluable publishing advice.

Mission: Wolf near Westcliffe, Colorado, for the opportunity to photograph their marvelous wolves. Wolves are amazing creatures that deserve our love and protection.

My brothers Dornie and Scott, and with loving memory of those who have left us - Mom, Dad and Merry, for their continuous love and support throughout my life.

About the Author

Mark Dornblaser grew up in Edina, Minnesota, the son of a university professor and an artist/writer. His family spent vacations backpacking, canoeing, or car camping in their station wagon, across all fifty states. These family trips instilled in him a love of nature, which led him to an undergraduate degree in Environmental Studies from Middlebury College and a Master's Degree in Oceanography from the State University of New York. Post-graduation, Mark worked as an environmental researcher at the Marine Biological Laboratory in Woods Hole, Massachusetts. His job included SCUBA diving for sediment cores in the cold lakes of Nova Scotia, Ontario, Massachusetts, Wisconsin, and Alaska.

Mark married his wife Deb in 1997 and they moved to Colorado, where he began working for the U.S. Geological Survey in Boulder. While with the USGS, Mark studied greenhouse gas emissions from rivers including the Mississippi and Columbia, and boated down nearly the entire length of the Yukon River in Alaska and Canada.

Always the adventurer, Mark has been to all seven continents, camera in tow. He has (briefly) flown a Cessna, a helicopter, a soar plane, and a hang glider, and has jumped out of a plane a couple times (with a parachute). He has sailed the North Atlantic in a 120' schooner, chartered sailboats with friends in the Caribbean and San Juan Islands, and even tried his hand at ice boating on a frozen lake in Colorado.

Mark received his first camera, a Kodak Instamatic, when he was a teen. He has been a photographer ever since, graduating to slide film and finally to digital. His photographs have appeared in Discover, Gourmet, The Boston Globe, Cape Cod Life, and Middlebury Magazine, and he has exhibited in galleries in New York, Connecticut, and Colorado. He began writing in earnest in his twenties, publishing travel articles and personal essays before turning to poetry. His poems have appeared in the Poetry Society of Colorado Annual.

Mark lives with his wife Deb in Louisville, Colorado.

www.ingramcontent.com/pod-product-compliance
Lightning Source LLC
Chambersburg PA
CBHW042107030726
47599CB00002B/145